Art and Commerce in the Dutch Golden Age

Art and Commerce in the Dutch Golden Age

Michael North

Translated by
Catherine Hill

Yale University Press
New Haven and London

Designed by Laura Church
Set in Baskerville by Best-set Typesetter Ltd, Hong Kong
Printed in Hong Kong

Library of Congress Cataloging-in-Publication Data

North, Michael, 1954–
    Art and Commerce in the Dutch Golden Age/ Michael North.
      p. cm.
    Includes bibliographical references and index
    ISBN 0–300–05894–2 (cloth)
    1. Painting, Dutch. 2. Painting, Modern—17th–18th centuries—
Netherlands. 3. Art and Society—Netherlands History 17th
century. 4. Netherlands—Social Conditions. I. Title
ND646.N67 1997
759.9492′09′032—dc20   96-46135
                                                          CIP

A catalogue record for this book is available from
The British Library

For Johannes and Jacobus

Contents

Preface

The decision to write this book arose from the lectures that I gave on Dutch history and art history at the University of Kiel. I was inspired by the discussions that took place with students of history of art and Dutch studies. During the summer semester of 1991 I substituted for Professor Sidney Pollard at the University of Bielefeld, and because I was able to take advantage of the services of his excellent staff, I finished writing in a relatively short period of time. The German edition of this book was published in 1992. The English edition has taken somewhat longer to prepare, its progress having been observed by me from the University of Greifswald, where I have taught since 1995.

A German historian treads on the foreign territory of the history of art or Dutch history in general only if he has the support of colleagues who are 'at home' in this area; I would therefore like to thank Professor Wim Blockmans, Professor Peter Klein and Dr Eric Sluijter in Leiden, as well as Professor Karel Davids in Amsterdam and Professor Herman Van der Wee in Leuven, for their many valuable suggestions. I am particularly grateful to Professor John Michael Montias of Yale University and Dr Martin Jan Bok in Utrecht for sharing their extensive knowledge of the social history of Dutch art. Last but not least, I am indebted to Catherine Hill in Kiel for the English translation and to Laura Church of Yale University Press for her careful copy-editing.

This book is dedicated to my young sons, Johannes and Jacobus, who were born while it was being written.

Michael North
Greifswald, May 1996

A note on monetary equivalents

1 guilder = 20 stuivers
1 Flemish pound = 6 guilders
1 ducat = 5 guilders

Introduction

In the seventeenth century the Netherlands was a country of superlatives: every year 70,000 pictures were painted, 110,000 lengths of cloth were produced and the gross national income was 200 million guilders. Dutch society was the most urbanized in Europe and the country had the highest literacy rate; an unusually large number of people owned works of art, the social infrastructure was well developed and various religious beliefs were tolerated. These are just some of the characteristics that made the Netherlands so unique during this period.

Following the Eighty Years War against Spain (1568–1648), the Netherlands emerged as a leading world power and trading nation, at a time when the European power structure had begun to change drastically: the economic and political centre of the modern world had finally moved from the Mediterranean to the North Sea and the Atlantic. Changes in trade, society and art took place against this background, beginning in the province of Holland and then spreading throughout the Netherlands. This period, which became known as the 'Golden Age', has fascinated historians and art historians ever since. Seventeenth-century Dutch painting is the most obvious manifestation of all the changes that took place during the Golden Age.

This study investigates the developments that took place in economic, social and artistic areas, as well as the way these areas interacted. At the same time, I have attempted to give a general overview of the history of art and of the social and economic developments in the Netherlands. This synthesis has been made possible by numerous detailed studies which have been carried out over the past two decades. This is the first time that the findings of these studies have been presented to a wider readership.

1   Pieter de Hooch, *The Mother*, c. 1661–3, Berlin, Gemäldegalerie Staatliche
Museen Preußischer Kulturbesitz. (Photo: J. P. Anders)

I

Historical Interpretations of Dutch Painting

The history of the reception of seventeenth-century Dutch painting is inextricably linked with the name of Georg Wilhelm
Friedrich Hegel, who was one of the first people to examine
various aspects of Dutch painting. In his *Aesthetics: Lectures on Fine
Art*, he wrote that,

> the Dutch had converted to Protestantism and had overcome
> the Spanish despotism of Church and Crown. The Dutch politi-
> cal landscape was not defined by an aristocracy which had
> expelled its prince and tyrant or imposed laws on him, nor a
> population made up of farmers and oppressed peasants, who,
> like the Swiss, revolted in order to acquire freedom. On the
> contrary, apart from the brave soldiers on land and the coura-
> geous seamen, most of the people were urban townspeople,
> well-off burghers who were involved in trading and who were
> not particularly pretentious, despite their comfortable lifestyle.
> However, when it was a question of fighting to preserve their
> well-earned rights, or the special privileges due to their prov-
> inces, cities, and corporations, they were prepared to revolt,
> bolstered by their firm faith in God and in their own courage
> and intelligence; and were unafraid of exposing themselves to
> any kind of danger whatsoever, despite the fact that the Spanish
> dominated half the world. They were quite prepared to shed
> their blood, and as a result of their courage and endurance they
> won both civil and religious independence for themselves . . .
> These sensitive and artistically endowed people wanted to use
> their painting to delight in this satisfying, and comfortable
> existence which was as powerful as it was just. In their pictures
> they wanted to relish once more, in every possible situation, in
> the neatness of their cities, houses, furnishings and domestic

peace, as well as their wealth, the respectable dress of their wives and children, the brilliance of their civil and political festivals, the courage of their seamen, the fame of their commerce and the ships that sailed the oceans of the world. The Dutch painters also brought a sense of honest and cheerful existence to objects in nature. All their paintings are executed meticulously and combine a supreme freedom of artistic composition with a fine feeling for incidentals. Their subjects are treated both freely and faithfully, and they obviously loved the ephemeral. Their view was fresh and they concentrated intensely on the tiniest and most limited of things.[1]

On the one hand, Hegel related the painter's art directly to nature and used the concept of Realism to define Dutch painting, which itself mirrored reality. On the other hand, he was the first person to attempt to interpret Dutch painting from an artistic and a sociological point of view by identifying the social conditions that influenced its development: the secular nature of the fundamental elements that explain the uniqueness of Dutch painting – Dutch agriculture, the battle of the Dutch against the sea, the fishermen, the sailors, the merchants, the dominance of the middle class and the Calvinist religion – was shown to contrast sharply with the Catholic culture of the aristocracy.[2] Thus Hegel can be seen as the father of the two most important approaches to Dutch painting, the realist and the sociological. While the theorists of Realism investigated the ways in which nature was represented in Dutch painting, the art sociologists discussed the prerequisites for the creation and development of a certain style.

Hegel was not the first to promulgate the concept of Realism in Dutch painting. He was able to refer to Samuel van Hoogstraeten who, in his *Inleyding tot de Hooge Schoole der Schilder-konst* (1678), wrote that 'a finished picture is like a mirror held up to nature, which simulates things that are not there, and we can see something praiseworthy and enjoyable in the way in which it deceives us'.[3] A picture could perform tasks other than the 'illusionistic representation'[4] of nature, but nineteenth-century writers on art associated only this feature with Dutch painting.

The image of Dutch painting has been influenced by German writing on the history of art, as well as by the nineteenth-century

French debate about Realism – the *bataille réaliste* – which was concerned with both art and literature. The conservative critic Gustave Merlet compared Flaubert's works with 'primitive' Dutch painting ('you would think you had been set down in a Flemish or Dutch museum'); whereas the liberal cultural theorist Théophile Thoré showed how much he appreciated the art of George Sand, by saying that he considered her work to be better than that of the Dutch artist Meindert Hobbema.[5] Thoré, the cultural philosopher Hippolyte Taine and the painter and writer Eugène Fromentin thought that the Dutch school was the historical foundation for the art of their own time. Thoré rediscovered Vermeer, analysed the themes of Dutch painting and was, simultaneously, preparing the way for the French naturalist and impressionist schools to represent everyday subjects in their art. The Dutch painters

> presented the lives of their compatriots . . . both inside their houses and in public places; on canals, country roads, water and land, under trees and on river banks. [They depicted] horsemen, hunters, sailors and fishermen, burghers and merchants, shepherds and charcoal burners, farmers and craftsmen, musicians and rogues, women with their children (those who had them) in the bosom of their family, at the fun of the fair, in the bustle of the tavern, working in the fields, as well as at respectable gatherings and meetings – in all occupations and diversions of life. Where could anyone find a more conscientious, innocent, uplifting and livelier history of any people than in these painted histories of customs and actions. This art described a period of Dutch history and thus a specific episode in the history of mankind.[6]

Thoré stimulated the revival of interest in Dutch painting and must therefore be regarded as influential upon the art of his time. Courbet closely modelled his scenes of everyday life in mid-nineteenth-century France on seventeenth-century Dutch examples. Even Degas admitted that he had found his painting style on the *route de Hollande*.[7]

Fromentin was also influential. His writings, perhaps more than those of anyone else, were informed by the concept of Realism that he found in Dutch painting: 'Why did a Dutch painter paint? he did not have to; and, we may note, he was never asked why he painted. A farmer with a wine-red nose looks at us with his big eyes and laughs, showing us all his teeth while he turns a spit: when the thing is well painted it is valuable in its own right.'[8] Thus, according to Fromentin, the Dutch painter depicted his surroundings realistically, and that is what he was paid for.

In Germany, Hegel's successors also referred to Dutch Realism in their discussion of art. Gustav Friedrich Hotho, for example, in his influential *Geschichte der deutschen und niederländischen Malerei* of 1842, contrasted the Dutch painters who presented the 'transitory and the indifferent' in their 'inexhaustible variety' with the Düsseldorf School and their 'sublime Madonnas and pale angels'.[9] However, in the following period, the debate became more objective, as art historians studied the different genres of Dutch painting in more detail. Some tried to establish the realism of certain genres, such as the group portraits;[10] others were more concerned with interpreting subject-matter and allied themselves to Aby Warburg's iconological method, by which, using contemporary literary sources, he had linked Botticelli's *Spring* and *Birth of Venus* to the reception of classical themes in the early Renaissance.[11] In this vein, the other great iconologist, Erwin Panofsky, interpreted Rembrandt's *Danäe* by reconstructing the pictorial tradition of the Danäe myth.[12] From here it is only a small step to questioning the dominant view that genre painting reflects seventeenth-century reality. Art historians were, in fact, looking for hidden meanings behind the realistic representation of everyday life. Hans Kauffmann decoded the motif of the Five Senses, which was widely used in numerous genre paintings (which were turned into prints during the sixteenth century), and Herbert Rudolph suggested that Vermeer's *Woman with a Balance* was in fact vanitas, a reminder of the transience of life[13] – an interpretation that has since been discredited. Sturla Gudlaugsson in her *Ikonographische Studien über die holländische Malerei und das Theater des 17. Jahrhunderts* deduced from the costumes in Jan Steen's genre pictures that the figures represented characters from the contemporary theatre.[14]

By 1940, the iconological premise had been stretched to the point that, although the renowned Dutch cultural historian Johan Huizinga had emphasized the abundantly significant subject-matter of seventeenth-century Dutch paintings, he warned just as forcefully against over-interpretation of them:

> Another word about the meaning of objects in our art from the seventeenth century. The viewer must nowadays resist the temptation imposed on him by his modern consciousness, to see more and something else in the representation of objects than the artist can have intended. Part of the meaning of this art will always escape us. We cannot decipher all the hidden signs and allusions even with the most rigorous study. There is meaning behind every flower in a floral painting. In still lifes every object has an emblematic meaning as well as its innate one. The same is true, to a certain incomprehensible extent, of the market trader whose messenger brings a letter from the music-making society that has so often been chosen as a much-loved subject in our painting or engraving.[15]

A few years later, after the Second World War, Ingmar Bergström wrote about Dutch still lifes in a similar way.[16] However, he was, in a sense, preaching to the converted, since by then historians no longer disputed the fact that still-life paintings contain symbolic meaning.

What exactly is a genre painting? The Utrecht School of Eddy de Jongh – which has influenced the study of Dutch seventeenth-century painting since the 1960s – has been the most vigorous participant in this debate. De Jongh and his students no longer speak of a 'Dutch reality' being represented in the paintings, but rather of hidden levels of meaning that can be decoded using emblematic literature. In the light of this interpretation, the task of genre painting was to help ordinary people to understand the moral content hidden beneath the beautiful, realistic façades. Accordingly, the title of the 1976 exhibition in the Rijksmuseum, Amsterdam, organized by the Utrecht School was, *Tot lering en vermaak* ('To teach and to entertain'). To clarify his argument, de Jongh coined the term *realisme–schijnrealisme* (realism–surface realism), separating the realistic form from the superficially realistic content of pictures: 'In numerous paintings objects are used to represent both what they are and something else. They indicate something beyond the picture itself. This phenomenon never affects the depiction as a whole, but, at most, certain specific details; however, objects which are not encoded and simply represent what they depict, also appear.'[17] The hidden messages can be deciphered by referring to the seventeenth-century emblematic literature that was available to the painters of the day.

Apart from Cesare Ripa's *Iconologia* (translated into Dutch in 1644), the Dutch had a rich emblematic tradition which could be found in Jacob Cats's emblem book. The epigrams (*sinnepoppen*) of Cats's book, written in verse form and accompanied by pictures, were not always understandable at first glance.[18] The central question of the present-day debate about Realism, is whether someone looking at a genre scene in the seventeenth century would have understood any of the references that it contained. When, for example, a picture depicted a bird-seller at a market offering a female customer a bird, or a hunter bringing his girlfriend a bird from the hunt, this would have been understood to mean that he wanted to sleep with her, since the verb *vogelen*, taken from the word *vogel* (bird), means to have sexual intercourse with someone.[19] However, if the content of a picture has to be decoded by means of emblems, then this says more about the erudition of the historian than about the level of sophistication of the painter and his audience, and the interpretation is less convincing.

It was only a question of time before de Jongh's hair-splitting followers attracted criticism. The critics – among them Lyckle de Vries, Peter Hecht and Eric Sluijter – on the one hand hit out against the term *realisme–schijnrealisme* and on the other accused de Jongh of not paying enough attention to the painters and the viewers in his interpretation of the paintings. The term *schijnrealisme* was a poor choice since it proceeds from a false premise: Dutch Realism does not mirror reality perfectly anyway.[20] Even the popular window motif, the *doorkikje*, and van Goyen's landscapes were painted in the studio and not from life. Critics such as Eric Sluijter also placed more emphasis on the painters' use of established motifs. Artists could evoke associations by their choice of motifs from specific painting traditions, in which well-known stereotypes are depicted and metaphors are expressed visually. The people who bought the pictures were able to interpret these motifs according to their own intellectual, social and

2   Gabriel Metsu, *The Hunter's Present*, c. 1665, Amsterdam, Rijksmuseum,
© Rijksmuseum Stichting.

religious backgrounds.[21] By using certain motifs, the painter could
express such concepts as the transience of earthly beauty and
could make them accessible to the viewer, even if the viewer did
not know enough about the particular emblems to be able to
decode them in the picture.

This careful linking of form and subject-matter, which was
used to reconstruct the artistic tradition, had a decisive effect on
the reception of Dutch painting in the 1980s, even though this
has since been overshadowed by Svetlana Alpers's spectacular
study *The Art of Describing*.[22] In her book, Alpers set herself against

the emblematic school. She investigated the relationship of painting
to science, cartography and optics and thus developed a visual
culture for the era. The task of Dutch painters was to depict reality
as they saw it, based on this visual culture. The painter's skill lay in
constructing the surface of a picture in such a way that the viewer
would see what the painter had experienced. Alpers did, however,
recognize the presence of symbols and literary references, but
wanted to have these deciphered by the viewer looking at the
painting, rather than by astute intellectual processes.[23]

Post-Hegel, the iconological approach to Dutch painting was
more popular than the sociological. This could have been
because the sociological approach to studying art was born in the
twentieth century, and for a long time dealt almost exclusively
with the Italian Renaissance. Since it was the study of Renaissance
art using the sociological framework that influenced the reception of seventeenth-century Dutch painting, the ways in which
Renaissance art was interpreted need to be considered.

There are three different approaches within the sociological
interpretation of art: the macro-sociological, micro-sociological
and the economic. Macro-sociologists investigate the development of European society and in so doing place certain phenomena in art (for example, the Italian Renaissance) in context. By
way of contrast, the central premise of the micro-sociological
approach is 'the changing material conditions under which art
was commissioned and created in the past'.[24] Among other things,
this includes examining the painter's training, the organiszation
of the guilds, and the relationship between painter and client.
Finally, the economic approach involves searching for links
between the art produced within a particular period of history
and the contemporary economy.

The macro-sociological interpretation of art history first
appeared in Alfred von Martin's *Soziologie der Renaissance* of 1932.[25]
Martin considered the Renaissance to be a 'middle-class revolution' in which the rational middle-class merchant ousted the aristocracy and the clerics from their social positions, thus allowing a
rational view of the world to come to the fore. Frederick Antal's
Florentine Painting and its Social Background, which appeared a little
later, has been even more influential in the interpretation of the
Renaissance.[26] Antal used the Florentine painters Gentile da

3   Gerrit Dou, *Young Woman with Boy at a the Window*, 1652, Karlsruhe, Staatliche Kunsthalle.

Fabriano and Masaccio to point up the differences between two social groups within the Florentine upper middle class who were purchasing art in the fifteenth century. The dynamic social climber commissioned the innovative Masaccio, while the overwhelmingly conservative majority of the upper middle class preferred the more traditional paintings of Fabriano. Thus, according to Antal, 'both the greater and the lesser artists were more concerned with catering for the expectations and preferences of the social classes than in developing artistically'.[27]

Two of Antal's disciples – Victor-Lucien Tapié and Arnold Hauser – applied the macro-sociological approach to both French Baroque art and art history in general. In *Baroque et classicisme*, Tapié identified Baroque art with an agricultural and aristocratic society, and contrasted its style with the classicism of a commercial and bourgeois world.[28] Hauser's *Social History of Art* is even more wide-ranging, stretching as it does from the Stone Age to modern film. Hauser also believes that the aristocratic and middle-class societies explain important developments in modern art: 'The principles of unity which now become authoritative in art, the unification of space and the unified standards of proportions [in Renaissance art] . . . are creations of the same spirit which makes its way in the organization of labour, in trading methods, the credit system and double-entry book-keeping.'[29] Hauser supported his thesis further by referring specifically to the Netherlands: 'In no period of the history of art is the sociological analysis of developments more rewarding than here, when two such basically different trends as Flemish and Dutch Baroque arise almost simultaneously, in close geographical proximity under quite similar external conditions.'[30] 'In the South foreign rule led to the victory of court culture over urban middle-class culture, whilst in the North the achievement of national independence meant the preservation of bourgeois culture.'[31] As the urban society grew, bourgeois naturalism, whose principal concern was to present the environment in its everyday guise became more acceptable.

Thus the nineteenth-century term 'Realism' took on a new sociological dimension in Hauser's work. His arguments were not, however, new. They had already appeared in 1926 in a little-known essay by the Soviet art historian Šelly Rosenthal, who tried to use the different social origins of the artists to explain the alternative ways in which Flemish and Dutch painting developed.[32] In terms of class, the artist's origins were as varied as the public's taste. While Flemish painters came from the rich middle class, Dutch painters generally came from the artisan milieu. The different tastes of art lovers in the south and the north of the Netherlands was even more marked. Since according to Montias 'each epoch represents itself as it wants to appear', the feudal structure in Flanders called for 'heroization', while the bourgeoisie inclined toward 'realism and corporeality'.[33] Eric Larsen, who tried to do nothing less than explain the 'relationship between art and capitalism in the Dutch Republic', considered the term Realism to be crucially important.[34] Larsen, taking Max Weber's *Protestantische Ethik* as his starting point, drew a direct line from Calvinism to Capitalism. Using the theory that creativity arises from certain conditions, he tried to explain the external causes of specific stylistic developments. For example, in the case of the Netherlands these were 'the accumulation of capital in the hands of a large new stratum of traders and/or minor capitalists, and the influence exercised by them upon the art of their world'.[35] This art was, as one would expect, realistic and expressed 'the innermost psyche of the newly prosperous class'.[36]

Larsen, Hauser and Rosenthal all tried to explain Dutch painting from the point of view of supply and demand. According to their model, the development of style and subjects in Dutch painting was determined by the demands of bourgeois society, or of a social class, for a realistic representation of their world. However, this development can also be interpreted from the point of view of the supplier (the painter), considering that the painter's social origin influences his artistic output, and, consequently, the history of art. This aspect has been studied by the Leiden sociologist F. van Heek, who is the only Dutch scholar working on interpreting Dutch painting from a sociological perspective.[37]

Van Heek explained that the unique appearance of Dutch landscape painting was due to the cultural isolation of the Dutch painter in the seventeenth century. As painters were cut off both from the trends of European Baroque art and from the Dutch patricians who preferred the Baroque style, an original style of painting developed within a separate milieu of artisans. Dutch landscape painting lost some of its originality only at the end of the seventeenth century, when French artistic taste became more widespread in the Dutch Republic and thus brought the painters' detachment to an end. Although van Heek's hypothesis gave people food for thought, it was undermined by the fact that the upper classes hung landscapes by local painters on their walls. In J. L. Price's stimulating study on Dutch art and society in the seventeenth century, the chapter 'Painting – the Artist as Craftsman' is unconvincing for this very reason.[38] Price places too much emphasis on the painter's low social origin and the limited education of the customers, while at the same time reproaching the Dutch intelligentsia and the Regents for preferring the Italian and Flemish styles. Price's work displays the characteristic weakness of many macro-sociological syntheses: they do not stand up to being checked at source.

Because of this deficiency, Gombrich supported a micro-sociological examination of art history in his discussion of Hauser's book.[39] It is, however, preferable to look at Peter Burke's *Culture and Society in Renaissance Italy 1420–1540*. Burke uses a unique methodology to show how fruitful the link between macro-sociological reflection and micro-sociological analysis can be.[40] As well as investigating the artists' social origins, education, social status and their relationship to their clients and patrons, Burke also analysed the iconography of taste, the function of the works of art and the picture of the world that they provide. With regard to the connection between the bourgeoisie and Realism in the Renaissance, Burke stated that the urban craftsmen and the merchants 'made important contributions to culture; craftsmen because they form the milieu from which artists often come, merchants because (more particularly when they are on the point of turning into nobles) they are often quick to patronise new arts'.[41]

A purely micro-sociological approach was first applied to the Italian Renaissance. In the 1930s, Martin Wackernagel had already investigated the milieu of the Florentine painters[42] and had thus also looked at the studio, the client and the art market. Åke Bengtsson made the first comparable study for Dutch painting in his *Studies on the Rise of Realistic Painting in Holland 1610–1625* of 1952.[43] This dissertation focused on the economic and social considerations that influenced art in Haarlem, and on the stimulus that this gave Dutch landscape painting. Bengtsson first studied the economic development of Haarlem as a textile centre and the inhabitants' standards of living. By dividing up the population according to income and comparing income with the prices paid for pictures, he determined that only the top three income groups could have bought paintings from the local master-painters. Bengtsson also researched the painters' social origins: two-thirds of them came from families with a tradition of painting. However, he was unable to establish a direct relationship between the style of painting found in Haarlem and the social and artistic environment there.

Linda Stone-Ferrier was no more successful in her *Images of Textiles: The Weave of Seventeenth-Century Dutch Art and Society* of 1980.[44] The connection between, on the one hand, textile production and the demand for it and, on the other, Dutch painting, is unclear – even if the Dutch use of textiles is clearly shown in the contemporary paintings. Otherwise – apart from works and source publications on the history of the Guild of St Luke and on the way individual painters organized their studios – there are only two significant monographs that use a micro-sociological approach to illuminate the social history of seventeenth-century Dutch art. These two books, *Artists and Artisans in Delft* (1982) and *Vermeer and his Milieu* (1989), were written by the Yale economist John Michael Montias.[45] In his first source-intensive study, Montias researched the social origin, wealth and guild membership of both the artistic and artisan communities in Delft. He also reconstructed the increasing number of paintings by both Dutch and foreign artists in the collections of burghers in Delft. Thus Montias did some pioneering work in the study of the social history of Dutch painting, even though he did not manage to integrate this with the general social history of the Netherlands.

Montias's second book is a study of Vermeer's family. He studied five generations of the family, starting with Johannes Vermeer's grandparents and ending with his grandchildren. In this book Montias shows how – at a time when the average Dutch family had only two children – a large number of children (nine or ten of Vermeer's fifteen children survived childhood) could ruin even a successful and admired painter. While Vermeer's father, the tavern-owner and art dealer Reynier Jansz. Vos, known as Vermeer, who had had two children, increased the family's fortunes, Johannes Vermeer who fathered so many children, ended up appreciably lowering his family's social status.

Finally, the economic interpretation of art history should be considered. In this field, economic historians are mostly concerned with the link between artistic development and the economy itself. Towards the end of the eighteenth century, the English music historian Charles Burney wrote, 'All the arts seem to have been the companions, if not the produce, of successful commerce; and they will, in general, be found to have pursued the same course . . . that is, like commerce, they will be found, upon enquiry, to have appeared first in Italy; then in the Hanseatic towns; next in the Netherlands.'[46] Since then historians and art historians, referring to the Italian merchant republics in the quattrocento and cinquecento, have tacitly agreed that the fine arts flourish most under conditions of economic expansion and general prosperity. They were rather surprised when economic historians described the European late Middle Ages as a time of economic depression, removing the basis of the cultural flowering that took place during the Renaissance. In a lecture at the Metropolitan Museum of Art, New York, in 1953, Robert Lopez was the first to maintain that the Italian economy was at its most prosperous in the thirteenth century and not during the Renaissance and that this prosperity had not led to any noteworthy artistic achievements.[47] This led him to formulate the theory that hard times, that is, periods of depression, are more likely to stimulate investment in culture than periods of economic growth. During an economic boom people invest their money in profitable enterprises and industrial production, whereas they are prepared to invest in 'unproductive' commodities such as art and architecture only during a depression, when trade, industry and land are not very profitable. This Lopez Thesis, as it is known, not only triggered controversy about the historians' view of Italy and Italy's economic growth in the late Middle Ages, but also provided a new focus for the study of the relationship between the state of the economy and the arts.

The economic crisis in the late Middle Ages had very different effects on individual sectors of the economy. Italy's general economic development does not appear to have been as depressed as

Lopez and his followers thought. Arnold Esch believed that it is true that 'people have to have money available in order to be able to finance large, unproductive projects'.[48] Esch did not, however, wish to acknowledge the fact that economy had a direct effect on the arts: 'A high level of economic development was certainly a prerequisite for [artistic development]',[49] but it was not in itself sufficient, since otherwise Genoa, Milan and Venice ought to have developed artistically in the same way as Florence.

The relationship between art and the state of the economy has not been investigated only in terms of the Italian Renaissance. With the Lopez Thesis in mind, John Munro has analysed the economic and cultural development of Flanders and Brabant in the fifteenth century.[50] A similar analysis has been carried out with regard to the relationship between the economy and architecture in Latin America,[51] using churches as a prime example; although the phases of church building could be correlated only with the expansion of the non-Indian population – hardly an unexpected finding. Until now, no study has drawn parallels between the economic development of the Netherlands and Dutch painting in the seventeenth century. In *Cultuur en getal* (1986), Wilfried Brulez applied the relationship between the economy, society and culture to Dutch investment in art and culture; but he stressed the fact that the influence of art and culture on the economy was marginal. He argued that 'a flourishing economy is not necessary for culture to flourish and cultural stagnation cannot be explained by economic stagnation'.[52] This means that investment in cultural pursuits does not 'compensate significantly for an economic depression, and investments in a flourishing economy do not compete with investments in culture'.[53]

Brulez may well be right in insisting that the level of resources invested in the cultural sector has always been small in comparison with the investment needs of the economy. However, when one examines the connections between the state of the economy and cultural interests from the point of view of the demand for artistic products, they appear in a different light. Thus, if the élites are excluded, a broad private demand for works of art can occur only when the basic material needs of a large proportion of the population have been satisfied; and this is more likely to take place during periods of economic growth than in a depression.

A number of hypotheses about the relationship between art, society and the economy can be advanced, based on the various interpretations of Dutch seventeenth-century painting summarized here. In the following chapters I have analysed these hypotheses empirically, using a micro-sociological–economic approach. This approach combines the latest research into the social and economic history of painting with the general social development of the Netherlands, which makes it possible to verify the iconographic and macro-sociological theses in certain instances. In the two following chapters I comprehensively review the seventeenth-century Dutch economy and society, since their decisive roles have either been ignored or dealt with only superficially in previous studies of Dutch painting. Following these chapters is one on the origin, training and social status of the painter, examined in the light of the contemporary Dutch social history. I then reconstruct the art market in the Netherlands, and in a further chapter I endeavour to discover which pictures the Dutch hung in their houses by analysing the pictures owned by private individuals. This provides information about artistic taste and the function of works of art in Dutch households. Finally, I examine how commerce and art influenced each other, allowing the seventeenth century to become the Golden Age of both Dutch painting and commerce.

II

The Dutch Economy

During the Golden Age, the Dutch economy astounded contemporary observers, and it still fascinates historians today. How was such a small country with less than two million inhabitants and virtually no natural resources able to become a leading economic and world power? Contemporary observers, many of whom were English and were envious of the success of the Dutch, suggested numerous reasons. In 1728 Daniel Defoe, in his tract *A Plan of the English Commerce*, wrote: 'The Dutch are the carryers of the World, the middle persons in Trade, the Factors and Brokers of Europe; they buy to sell again, take in to send out; and the greatest part of their vast commerce consists in being supply'd from all parts of the World, that they may supply all the World again.'[1]

The English ambassadors to the Netherlands, William Temple and George Downing, also tried to explain the reasons behind the country's success. Temple finally attributed the economic development of the Netherlands to the fact that the country was very densely populated: 'I conceive the true origin and ground of trade to be great multitudes of people crowded into a small compass of land, whereby all things necessary to life are rendered dear, and all men who have possessions are induced to parsimony; but those who have none are forced to industry and labour. Bodies that are vigorous fall to labour; such as are not supply that defect by some sort of invention and ingenuity. These customs arise first from necessity and grow in time to be habitual in a country.'[2] Downing, however, attributed the growth of the Dutch trading power to the herring trade: 'The herring trade is the cause of the salt trade, and the herring and salt trade are the causes of this country's having, in a manner, wholly engrossed the trade of the Baltic Sea for they have these bulky goods to load their ships with thither.'[3] Even though herrings were described as the 'golden food' of the Dutch and the Baltic trade, as the country's mother trade (*moedercommercie*), it would not be true to say that the Dutch economy was based solely on the herring trade. In order to explain the unparalleled growth in the Dutch economy at a time when, in general, Europe was in a period of economic crisis, it is necessary to look at the various sectors of the economy, and the internal and external factors that shaped it.

Let us first look at the growth in the population to which William Temple referred:

Table 1 The population in millions of the Netherlands 1500–1795[4]	
1500	0.9–1
1550	1.2–1.3
1600	1.4–1.6
1650	1.85–1.95
1750	1.85–1.95
1795	2.078 (Census)

The Dutch population grew continuously during the sixteenth and the first half of the seventeenth century; by 1650 it had doubled in size. Over the one hundred years that followed, the size of the population stagnated and in many regions it actually decreased. Taking the province of Holland as an example, the urban population increased more than the rural population. At the beginning of the sixteenth century, half of the provincial population lived in cities; by 1622, this had reached fifty-nine per cent; and in 1795, sixty-three per cent.[5] By the middle of the seventeenth century, when the population growth was less rapid, Holland was the most densely populated and most urbanized province in western Europe. The port cities of Rotterdam and Amsterdam grew more quickly – from 50,000 inhabitants (1600) to 200,000 (1650) – than the industrial cities of Haarlem, Delft and Gouda. An exception to this was Leiden, where textiles were produced and where the population increased suddenly, by about 70,000 inhabitants, in the middle of the seventeenth century. While most of the port cities also continued to grow in the second half of the century, there was a marked reduction in the population of the industrial centres, which clearly paralleled the industrial recession. The only port city that suffered the same fate was Enkhuizen, which was the centre of the herring trade.

Fig. 4   Population of the province of Holland 1514–1795 (from J. de Vries)

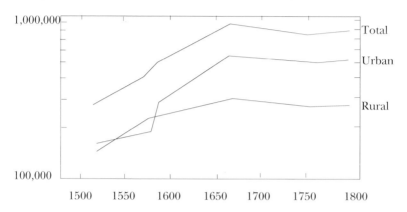

What caused these demographic changes? For a long time, experts thought that migration from the south of the Netherlands (the result of the Eighty Years War with Spain) was affecting the changes in the population most. However, according to van Houtte's estimates, it appears that no more than 80,000 people fled north from the Spanish troops.[6] Although these migrants were an important factor in the modernization of the northern provinces, whether in the Leiden textile industry or the Haarlem School of painting – especially given the many Germans who came to the Netherlands during the war – the number of migrants from the south was not enough in itself to explain the enormous demographic growth. Far more crucial was the fact that people married younger during the first half of the seventeenth century and were therefore likely to have more children – leading to an increase in the birth-rate. Research has revealed that brides in Amsterdam in 1626/7 were, on average, twenty-four years old, while in the second half of the seventeenth century and in the eighteenth century they were twenty-six and a half years old (1676/7) or twenty-seven years and two months old (1726/7)

respectively.[7] The increase in the age at which people married, in the second half of the seventeenth and in the eighteenth century resulted inevitably in a reduction in the birth-rate. Thus the Netherlands, owing to its particularly extensive urbanization and the high rate of mortality associated with this, depended on a high rural birth-rate and on a continual migration to the cities. Jan de Vries calculated that Amsterdam alone needed 1,700 migrants every year in order to maintain its population at 200,000, since the mortality-rate clearly outstripped the urban birth-rate.[8] If the birth-rate in the rural areas that supplied migrants for the cities declined, this had a negative effect on the growth of the country's population as a whole. However, in general, the demographic growth in areas that did not contribute to migration of people to the cities, such as remote agricultural regions like Overijssel, con-tributed to the overall stability of the population in the Nether-lands. The total economic development also influenced the size of population, that is, the size of the work-force involved in production, and the purchasing power of the consumers. This phenomenon is looked at in more detail when consideration is given to the various sectors of the Dutch economy.

Agriculture and fishing formed the primary sector of the economy in the seventeenth century. Dutch agriculture was mod-ernized and commercialized: new crops and agricultural tech-niques raised levels of production so that they were in line with market demands; and cheap grain was imported annually from the Baltic region in large quantities. According to estimates by Jan de Vries, about 60,000 lasts (120,000 tons) of imported grain fed about 600,000 people, that is, about a third of the Dutch popula-tion.[9] Importing the grain, which would have been expensive and time consuming for the Dutch to have produced themselves, kept the price of grain low and thus stimulated individual demand for other foodstuffs and consumer goods. Apart from this, being able to give up labour-intensive grain production freed both the land and the work-force for more productive agricultural divisions. The peasants specialized in livestock husbandry and dairy farming as well as in cultivating industrial crops and fodder crops; flax, madder and rape were grown, as were tobacco, hops and turnips. These products were bought mostly by urban businesses. There was also a demand among urban consumers for dairy products such as butter and cheese which, in the sixteenth century, became more expensive than grain. The high prices encouraged the peasants to improve their animal husbandry techniques, for example, they began feeding their animals indoors in order to raise the milk yield of their cows.

As well as dairy farming and cultivating industrial crops, a third sector reflected the way in which agriculture was being modernized – horticulture. In the sixteenth century, fruit and vegetables were to be found only in gardens belonging to the upper classes. This changed in the early part of the seventeenth century when horticulture became accepted as an agricultural sector. Whole villages began to cultivate fruit and vegetables.[10] The villages in Streek, between Hoorn and Enkhuizen, specialized in cabbages and carrots; the Langedijk, north of Alkmaar, was famous for onions, mustard and coriander; other villages produced fruit and vegetables and cultivated trees in nurseries. The produce was then transported by water to markets in the cities, where the consumption of fruit and vegetables was no longer restricted to the upper class. As the demand for agricultural produce from both consumers and industry increased, agricultural land became more valuable and people tried to work the available land more intensively and to reclaim more land. In order to increase production on existing land, the peasants made more use of crop rotation and, in particular, began to apply dung to the soil regularly, rather than leaving the fertilization process up to the grazing livestock. For the first time industrial waste, such as ash from the soap-boilers, was collected in the cities and sold in the country as 'artificial fertilizer'. The increased yield and price of land justified poldering and draining even more land.

The Dutch battle against the sea is legendary. Noorderkwartier in Holland, with its numerous lakes and stretches of water, was particularly suitable for land reclamation and one of the biggest projects undertaken there was the draining of the Beemster, which began in 1608.[11] The richest merchants in Amsterdam contributed 1,492,500 guilders to reclaim a good 7,100 hectares of land. Forty-three windmills powered the drainage pumps so that they were able to lease the polder as early as 1612. The 123 investors received annual leasing payments of about 250,000 guilders which was equal to an interest rate of seventeen per cent.

5   Anonymous, *Polder near Enkhuizen*, c. 1600, Enkhuizen, Town Hall.

Land reclamation continued, and between 1590 and 1665 almost 100,000 hectares were reclaimed from the wetland areas of Holland, Zeeland and Friesland. However, land reclamation decreased significantly after the middle of the seventeenth century because the price of agricultural products began to fall, making land reclamation far less profitable in the second part of the century. Dutch agriculture was finally affected by the general agricultural crisis in Europe during the last two decades of the seventeenth century. However, what is astonishing about this is not that Dutch agriculture was affected by critical phenomena such as a decrease in sales and production, but the fact that the crisis appeared only relatively late in Dutch agriculture. In Europe as a whole, the exceptional reduction in the population and the related fall in demand for grain since the beginning of the seventeenth century had caused the price of agricultural products to fall.[12] Dutch peasants were able to remain unaffected by this crisis for a long time because they had specialized in dairy farming, industrial crops and horticulture. However, towards the end of the seventeenth century they too were overtaken by the general agricultural crisis.

How significant is Dutch agriculture as a yardstick for measuring the country's general economic development? As a rule, a country's agriculture is judged by its ability to feed a growing sector of the population which, in the main, is no longer employed in farming – that is, whether it aids or hinders growth in the non-agricultural sectors of the economy. However, grain was imported so the increased levels of Dutch agriculture were supplying only some of the needs of the population. Apart from supplying industry with raw materials, agriculture seems to have influenced economic development indirectly, but this does not mean that it was any less intensive. The result of specializing in various agricultural sectors was that only a relatively small section of the population, about thirty per cent in the country as a whole – in the province of Holland it was only twenty per cent – had to work on the land. Thus advances in agriculture freed the majority of the population for work in the growing industrial and service sectors. Dutch business and trade could not have grown as it did without a productive agricultural base and the comparatively modern way in which its work-force was organized. In addition, the economy was encouraged to develop in order to fulfil the demands of those involved in agriculture, since the prosperous peasants also wanted industrial products – luxury and imported goods such as furniture, clocks, jewellery, table silver and pictures.

Dutch herring fishing, which was praised by contemporaries, belongs to the primary sector of the economy since it utilizes the riches of the sea. However, it can be viewed as part of the secondary sector since it was also a processing industry. The Dutch caught the herring at sea, then treated and preserved them in imported salt, packed them in barrels made out of imported wood and exported the end-product.[13] In good years, Dutch fishermen caught more than 200 million herring, this was about half the total European herring catch. The most important market for Dutch herring was the Baltic region where the Dutch had what amounted to a monopoly in the herring trade. Other markets were the German North Sea coast, Cologne, the Rhine valley and Normandy, despite the fact that the latter had its own local fishermen.

Why were the Dutch fishermen so much more successful than other European fishing nations? The most important factor was that the Dutch could sell their catch less expensively with no concessions in quality, owing to the superior technology that they employed in catching and processing the fish. The Dutch were able to preserve the herring catch on board ship and therefore did not have to bring it back to land for processing.[14] That gave their ships, the *bussen*, which had been specially designed for herring fishing, a greater range than their European competitors. The Dutch were no longer restricted to the coastal fishing grounds, they were also able to harvest the teeming deep-water fishing grounds near Scotland, Iceland and the Shetlands. Also, the herring fleet was accompanied by armed war ships to protect them against pirates and enemy warships. Herring fishing, processing and selling was supervised by the Board of Directors of the Main Fishery, *College van Commissarissen van de Groote Visscherij*, which acted like a cartel, it established quotas and the market price; its sole purpose was to dominate the European market.[15] Pressure was put on Dutch sales in the second half of the seventeenth century, once the foreign competitors started receiving state subsidies to help them to overcome their technological shortcomings in catching and processing the herring catch. While the competitors' production costs sank, the Dutch catch became more expensive due, in part, to the loss of up to 100 *bussen* as a result of the Anglo-Dutch wars.[16] Even though the Dutch attempted to keep the price of herring artificially high by cutting back their production levels, they succeeded only in reducing their share of the market.

The Dutch were also extensively involved in whaling. Whale bones were turned into combs, hair-clasps, buttons and corset bones, but whaling was particularly important for obtaining train oil. Train oil was extracted by rendering down the blubber and was in demand particularly as lamp oil, it was also used as a raw material in soap-boiling. In the course of the seventeenth century, the growing need for train oil led to a considerable increase in whaling. In the first decade of the seventeenth century only about twenty whalers worked the Spitzbergen coast and Jan Mayen Island each year, by the second half of the century the numbers had increased to between one and two hundred whalers working the waters of the Greenland Sea each year.[17] Whaling was an industry that gave employment to the inhabitants of the Dutch and German North Sea coasts. Nowadays the gravestones on the islands of Föhr and Amrum record the names of the North Frisian whaling captains who worked for the Dutch.

The secondary sector of the economy was shaped by the many contemporary crafts and industries in the Netherlands. The majority of the working population in the seventeenth century worked in industry and thus in the secondary sector – in the province of Holland for example, this amounted to about forty per cent of the working population.[18] The textile industry was the most important and was built up during the latter part of the sixteenth century having been started in Holland by the Flemish and Brabantine émigrés. The refugees brought the progressive textile industry with them to Leiden and Haarlem and ensured the dominance of Dutch textiles on the world market.[19] The Dutch textile industry was especially successful in dyeing and finishing textiles, both of which were highly profitable. For example, as well as bleaching linen from Flanders, France and Germany in Haarlem, Dutch cloth-makers were able to make a forty-seven per cent profit by dyeing and finishing the undyed, semi-finished cloth that came from England.[20] This really stuck in the English manufacturers' throats and in 1614 a group of London merchants led by Alderman Cockayne forced the king to forbid the export of white cloth.[21] The Dutch countered this by banning the export of finished products and the English king in turn retaliated by imposing a ban on wool exports. The end result of all this, however, was that the English exports fell by a third so that the ban had to be lifted in 1617. Since none of the plants used to dye cloth were grown in England, it was much more expensive to dye cloth in England than in Holland.

An important innovation in textiles was the manufacture (in Leiden) of *nieuwe draperies* (new drapery), a light-weight cloth. In the first half of the seventeenth century, light worsted, bays, says, fustian etc., were produced in large amounts – more than 100,000 lengths a year.[22] However, in the second half of the century the Leiden producers with their lightweight cloth lost ground. The worsteds in particular caused the *nieuwe draperies* to be 'pushed to the wall by the competition from England since theirs was not only a better raw material but also a cheaper one as long as a rural work-force was available'.[23] The Dutch textile industry, which was only partially based during rural areas, was able to reassert itself by producing the expensive camlet and the woollens of the *oude draperie* (old drapery or heavyweight cloth), which resulted in a growth in *oude draperie* during the 1730s. These high-quality products show that the Dutch were able to get hold of the necessary raw materials easily [the Turkish camel hair for the camlet, and Spanish wool for the woollens (*oude draperie*)], and that they knew how to use both indigo and cochineal to dye the cloth. The manufacturers in Leiden concentrated on satisfying the demand for high-quality textiles while the market for cheap, mass-produced cloth was lost to England. This change in the market was caused not only by the high wages and production costs, the Dutch position was also weakened by the ban on Dutch imports that was imposed by other European countries. The Dutch tried to overcome this disadvantage by changing from mass-producing cloth to finishing quality and luxury goods. This was when the silk processing began to increase in Amsterdam, Haarlem and Utrecht – an industry that would continue to flourish even when the industrial recession hit the Netherlands.

The other important national and international industry in the

Netherlands in the seventeenth century was shipbuilding. By developing numerous types of ship, the shipbuilders had, by the end of the sixteenth century, turned the Dutch into the leading European shipbuilding nation, a state of affairs that was to last for the next 150 years. One of the most successful ship designs was the *fluyt* which, according to popular myth, was first built in 1590 in Hoorn.[24] Dutch shipbuilders and shipping benefited greatly from the *fluyt*, which was built in large numbers to a standard design and was suitable for most of the different types of trade. Standardizing the shipbuilding process lowered the manufacturing costs. The running costs of the ships were also low, owing to use of technical equipment on board – such as the block and tackle – which meant that the crew size was reduced. An enormous shipbuilding industry grew up in Zaanstreek in Waterland, to the north of Amsterdam, which was instrumental in developing and refining mechanization and the division of labour in shipbuilding.

Towards the end of the century about six hundred sawmills and industrial mills were operating in the region as sub-contractors for constructing certain parts of the ships, such as blocks or masts.[25] Simultaneously, a whole army of ancillary industries – sail-makers, rope-makers, compass-makers – developed around the shipyards, which were no longer run as artisan businesses by individual carpenters, but as large family enterprises with a great deal of capital. In contrast to the independent urban master-carpenters who built ships, these firms concentrated on mass-producing ships. Unfortunately, they neglected to design and build new types of ship and this eventually meant that they lost their technological advantage in the area of shipbuilding, even though the shipyards' order books were full. Around the middle of the eighteenth century, the decrease in the number of yards and sawmills, as well as the reduction in the manufacture of sailcloth, testified to the fact that Holland was no longer Europe's shipyard.

Shipbuilding and the textile industry were not the only sectors in which the Dutch dominated Europe, they were also pre-eminent in the ceramic and foodstuff industries, which were linked to the export trade. The ceramic industry had a very diverse range of products, which were made from local clay and kaolin deposits to produce goods for export.[26] Clay pipes from Gouda were found all over Europe as smoking was becoming more and more popular.

In the second half of the seventeenth century, Delft faience, the first imitation of Chinese porcelain (which was not readily available on the European markets), acquired an international reputation. Its products would later stimulate the founding of other porcelain factories in neighbouring countries.

Although the Dutch brickmakers may not have been so spectacular, they were just as successful. At the beginning of the seventeenth century they were producing more than two hundred million bricks annually and were thus as productive as the English brick industry at the time of the Industrial Revolution.[27] The growth in brickmaking resulted from the increasing urbanization and the flourishing local building trade, bricks were also exported to the Baltic region as well as to the West and East Indies, since the ships used the bricks as ballast for their voyages. In the foodstuffs and luxury goods trade, beer-brewing, which had an excise duty imposed on it, experienced a downturn while the other sectors prospered, especially the processing and the re-exporting of imported foodstuffs. The expanding trade sectors included salt-making, sugar-refining and distilling.

Summarizing the development of Dutch industry shows that its leading position in Europe was based on four main factors: – its superior technology; its extensive use of sources of energy, for example, turf and wind; the adequate size of its work-force and readily available investment capital. Technological superiority, together with the way in which energy was used in production processes, gave Dutch products a competitive edge on the European market. However, this was to change in the late seventeenth and eighteenth centuries once the neighbouring countries used enormous state subsidies to catch up with the technological advantage that had been enjoyed by the Dutch. Once the difference in prices had been evened out, Dutch industry was at a severe disadvantage because of its wage costs, which were the highest in Europe.[28] In the Netherlands it was not really practicable to reduce costs by moving production to rural areas. Though home textile production had been developed around the Twente and in Brabant, both of which were less developed agriculturally, the high agricultural wages meant that industrial production in rural areas was much more expensive than in England, for example, where seventy to eighty per cent of the population were still employed in agriculture in 1688. Dutch industry could assert its position on the world market in the eighteenth century only by trading in quality and luxury products while losing its markets in general trade goods; this development was greatly influenced by the protectionist strategies employed in neighbouring countries.[29] Thus the number of people employed in industry declined, as did the importance of industrial production in the Dutch economy as a whole.

By the end of the seventeenth century, the tertiary, or service, sector had become the most important area and people working in this field had the highest incomes.[30] The tertiary sector was composed of the independent sectors of shipping, trade and finance. The co-operation that existed between these sectors led to the Netherlands' supremacy in world trade, and Amsterdam became the warehouse for trade goods from all over the world. Dutch ships collected goods from the regions where they were grown or produced, and supplied the markets where there was a demand for such goods. The Dutch ships were not only quicker but also 'cleaner, cheaper, and safer'[31] than those owned by their competitors. Clean, well-captained ships with well-fed crews increased the efficiency and the speed of transport by sea, lowered the risks and, consequently, the insurance costs. This meant that the Dutch were able to offer merchants and producers at home and abroad the lowest freight costs. The volume of goods shipped increased and, as the tonnage of the trade fleet increased (about 400,000 tonnes in 1670), so the freight rates fell.

Apart from this, the risks and costs of shipping were reduced by the introduction of divided ownership.[32] A ship could often have sixty owners; for example an Amsterdam shipowner who died in 1612 left behind shares in twenty-two ships, including a one-sixteenth share in thirteen ships, a one-thirty-second share in seven, as well as a one-seventeenth and a one-twenty-eighth share in others. The result of this was that both risk and ownership were evenly distributed, encouraging the middle classes to invest in shipping which meant, in turn, that the Dutch merchant fleet had another decisive cost advantage in international maritime transportation. Its costs were not only lower than those of the Hanseatic cities but also those of their nearest rival, England. More than half of all the goods from the Baltic region were brought to England on Dutch ships. The Dutch also dealt with most of the trade between England and its West Indian and the North American colonies, since the English did not possess either sufficient shipping tonnage or sailors.

Dutch foreign trade was based on the well-established trading links between Northern and Western Europe in an area that stretched from the British Isles in the west and Gibraltar in the south, to Bergen and the Gulf of Finland in the north and north-east. They sold the Baltic countries herring from the North Sea, salt from the Bay of Biscay, and wine from France as well as grain, wood and forestry products and industrial raw materials such as flax and hemp. Thus, in the second half of the sixteenth century, the Dutch ousted the Hanseatic cities from their role in western trade by concentrating on transporting grain, wood, herring and salt quickly and cheaply. In the 1580s, about half of Danzig's imports and exports were transported on Dutch ships and the Dutch share of the Baltic trade was expected to increase still further to encompass sixty to seventy per cent of the goods that were transported.[33]

The Dutch were justified in viewing the Baltic trade as a mother trade (*moedercommercie*). The grain imported from the Baltic region fed a large part of the population and, as has been shown, thus freed Dutch farmers to engage in more profitable sectors. Wood was used for shipbuilding and in industry as were its by-products – pitch, tar and ashes. This inexpensive supply of ship-building material including the flax and hemp for sails and ropes, and technical innovations, guaranteed the superiority of the Dutch shipyards and thus the low freight rates which Dutch shipping companies were able to offer. Herring processing also needed large amounts of prefabricated barrel staves from the Baltic region, while ash from Danzig and Königsberg was generally bought by other industries, such as the soap-boiling industry. Finally, the Baltic trade made it possible for the Netherlands to get a foot-hold in other trading areas.

By the end of the sixteenth century, the Dutch were able to use their monopoly in the Baltic grain trade to intensify their trade with southern Europe when the harvests failed in the west and south of Europe. Gradually, the range of goods involved in the Dutch Baltic trade changed.[34] The Baltic countries began to import high-quality goods such as spices, sugar, citrus and southern fruits and textiles as well as the customary salted herrings and wine. In effect, the Dutch controlled not only the export trade in grain and wood, but also imported finished western goods and luxury products. However, this import monopoly was eventually endangered by military disputes with Spain, which affected supplies; but these disputes, like the trade war with England, could only hinder Dutch trade with the Baltic in the short-term, since Denmark had granted Holland free access to the Baltic through the Sound. In the second half of the seventeenth century, however, the reduced demand for grain led to changes in western and southern Europe that manifested themselves in the grain trade with the Baltic.[35] The Dutch compensated for these losses by trading with Russia and overseas as well as by increasing the direct exchange between producers and consumers (the *vorbijlandvaert*), which circumvented the Amsterdam commodity markets. Taking the Netherlands' growing *vorbijlandvaert* into account, the Dutch Baltic trade remained stable in the long-term whether other nations (especially England and Denmark) increased their shipping in the Baltic or not.

The Dutch trade with the Mediterranean and the Levant was dependent on the state of their war with Spain. The first Dutch ship, which had silver worth 100,000 ducats on board to buy spices and silk in Aleppo, reached the Syrian coast in 1595.[36] The Venetian, French and English merchants in the Levant were annoyed even though this did not threaten their existing transit trade with Venice. Finally, the twelve-year truce between Spain and the Dutch Republic (1609–1621) enabled the Dutch to break into the Mediterranean trade. They transported goods – for example, Spanish salt and wool to Italy – and supplied the Mediterranean area with pepper and spices from the East Indies; they themselves bought cotton and Persian raw silk. After the truce, the Treaty of Westphalia (1648) opened up new opportunities for the Dutch in Mediterranean and Levantine trade once again. In the end, they controlled the trade in Spanish wool as well as in Turkish camel and goat's hair and were thus able to guarantee a constant supply of raw material for the woollens and camlet that were produced in Leiden; these products were then sold in the Mediterranean and in the Ottoman Empire.

However, the Dutch were able to dominate the area like this only until France's large-scale mercantile policy in the Mediterranean trade bore its first fruits. In the 1660s, Colbert enticed expert Dutch textile-makers to leave the Netherlands and succeeded in conjuring up a textile industry out of thin air in Languedoc, which produced fine cloth. Although production began slowly, towards the end of the seventeenth century the French products were dominating the market in the Ottoman Empire. The Dutch were unable to do anything to avoid this happening, especially since France was able to defend her newly won markets with a superior military presence in the Mediterranean.[37]

Although Dutch trade with the Mediterranean and the Levant benefited from periods of peace, such times also made overseas trade, especially with Africa and the West Indies, more difficult. Since Spain and Portugal had divided the world between them in the first part of the century, other countries could be successful in trade only if Spain and Portugal were involved in European wars and therefore neglecting their colonies; or if other countires were able to carry out plundering raids against Spain and Portugal themselves. The Dutch trade in the West Indies and Africa is inextricably bound up with the Dutch *West-Indische Compagnie* (WIC) which was founded in 1621 after the end of the cease-fire.[38] Like the VOC (*Verenigde Oost-Indische Compagnie*), which had been founded earlier, the aim of the WIC was to consolidate Dutch trade in the West Indies and above all to stop the Dutch trading companies that were operating in the area from competing with each other. The WIC was set up as a joint-stock company, a few merchants who had been involved in trading with the Caribbean, Brazil and Guinea for a long time, invested large sums of money in it and became directors of the company. It had been possible to amass the initial capital of about seven million guilders only because the people living in the cities that were not directly connected with shipping, for example Leiden, Utrecht, Dordrecht, Haarlem, Deventer, Arnhem and Groningen, were prepared to invest substantial sums in the new company.[39]

The WIC's initial success was modest, since their aim was to conquer the Spanish and Portuguese possessions the money disappeared quickly. The WIC would have been quickly forgotten if

Piet Heyn had not captured the Spanish silver fleet, arriving from Mexico, off the Cuban coast and thus added more than eleven million guilders into the WIC's coffers. In order to continue to expand financially, the WIC needed a solid commercial base in the New World in addition to importing gold from Africa. This was made possible when the sugar-growing centre of Pernambuco (Recife) in Brazil was conquered and the Portuguese were forced to retreat.[40] For the first time in history, the Dutch controlled the sugar trade and, as a result of this, the slave trade as well. Sugar-growers used slave labour, expanding the sugar production there-fore led to an unending stream of African slaves being brought into the country.

The Dutch exploitation of the Brazilian sugar crop came to an abrupt end in 1644, when a serious revolt broke out among the Brazilian sugar-growers; this resulted in the Dutch returning Brazil to Portugal for eight million guilders in 1661. By then, the WIC was deeply in debt and, in the second half of the century, limited the scope of its activities to supplying the West Indian colonies belonging to the other European powers, being involved in the slave trade and importing gold from their African colonies. The Dutch supplied the English and Spanish sugar-planters with the necessary workers and tools, and sugar production was increased using Dutch know-how and capital. The black popula-tion in the islands increased substantially – in Barbados from 5,680 (1645) to 82,023 (1667) – and more and more planters were in debt to Dutch traders.

Trade with Spanish America was carried out directly and indi-rectly via Spain and proved to be particularly profitable. This was where the Dutch earned the silver which they needed to purchase goods in the Baltic. The Dutch supplied Spanish America via Cadiz with woollens and camlet from Leiden in particular, and cinnamon from Ceylon. Between 1676 and 1689 the WIC also transported about 20,000 slaves, mainly to Curaçao and from there to the Spanish Caribbean.[41] The quasi-monopoly of the WIC in the slave trade with the Spanish colonies came to an end in 1679 and the Spanish planters then bought their slaves in the slave markets in the English colony of Jamaica. Owing to its con-venient location off the American coast, the Dutch island of Curaçao continued to remain the centre for trading with Latin

America, the Dutch supplied the country with linen, spices, wax candles, silk and paper.

Towards the end of the century, the Dutch suffered from increasing European competition both in transporting goods to the West Indies and the contingent trade with Africa. All the European countries were tempted by the trade in slaves, gold and ivory; and it was almost a matter of prestige to have a fort in West Africa. However, the Dutch were unable to maintain their supremacy in Guinea (which they had captured from the Portuguese) for long. While the competition with other European countries resulted in higher prices on the African slave markets, it also reduced the gold exports destined for the Netherlands.[42]

The Indian and South East Asian trade, which the Portuguese had viewed as their domain in the sixteenth century, became a flourishing sector of Dutch trade during the first half of the seventeenth century. After the first Dutch fleet (under the command of Cornelius de Houtmans) reached Java in 1595, the *voorcompagnien* from Holland and Zeeland formed a monopoly called the *Verenigde Oost-Indische Compagnie* (VOC).[43] The VOC was a chartered joint-stock company which was awarded sovereign rights by the States General and allowed to build forts, recruit soldiers and sign contracts with foreign rulers. The VOC was divided into six chambers (Amsterdam, Zeeland, Rotterdam, Delft, Hoorn and Enkhuizen) which built and equipped ships independently of each other, and sold the goods that they imported. Financial backers also invested money in the individual chambers although the Amsterdam chamber with its investment of 3,674,915 guilders supplied about half of the initial capital.[44] Soon people began to speculate in the shares and the stock and, in the course of the century, they were traded at well over their original value. The *bewindhebbers*, who were directors for life, headed the chambers and elected the executive committee, the *Heren XVII* (*XVII Gentlemen*), from among their number.

Matters in Asia were handled by a local governor general; his job was to ensure Dutch access to the spice markets using either diplomatic or military means. Pepper and rare spices grew in the Indonesian archipelago and on the Moluccas, thus the VOC needed a centre in the spice-growing area to enable them to influence the pepper and spice trade. This was the task assigned

6   Hendrick Vroom, *Peaceful Trading on the Indian Coast*, 1614, London, National Maritime Museum.

to the Governor General, Jan Pietersz. Coen. He founded the fort of Batavia near the harbour town of Bantam on Java – Batavia is now called Djakarta and is the capital of Indonesia. None the less, he had to deal with competition from the English which, however, was not as well funded and did not have such a high volume of trade. Coen's real aim was to break into the lucrative trade within Asia as the Portuguese, the Spanish and the English had done. Exclusive supply contracts were supposed to ensure a Dutch monopoly in cloves and nutmeg. If their partners did not observe the terms of their contract, the VOC killed and enslaved the spice producers and also destroyed some of the nutmeg and clove trees in order to keep the price high on the European market. The VOC tried very hard to penetrate the Portuguese system of forts in India because they wanted to take over the cinnamon market in Ceylon (which they succeeded in conquering in 1656), as well as the textile trade on the Coromandel Coast and in Bengal. Towards the end of the seventeenth century, cotton textiles and silk had replaced pepper as the VOC's main trade goods.[45]

Trading with Japan was also a lucrative business. The Dutch

founded a factory in Deshima off Nagasaki in 1641, after the Portuguese had finally been excluded from Japanese trade in 1639. The VOC imported silk, textiles, wool and sugar to Japan, while Japan supplied precious metals – silver, copper, and gold kobangs – which the VOC needed to buy goods in India and in the Indonesian archipelago. 13–15 million guilders of the silver that was needed for trading in Asia each decade came from Japan, 3–5 million from Persia and 8.4–8.8 million from the Netherlands.[46] The ban on exporting silver from Japan in 1668, and the decline in the trade with Japan drastically reduced the supply of silver which the VOC needed in order to trade in Asia. As a result, the VOC had to increase the amount of silver it imported from Europe. Since the trade between Europe and Asia was expanding continuously, and the textiles that were in demand in Europe as well as the new products – coffee and tea – could only be bought in Asia for silver, the Asian trade consumed more and more of the precious metal.

More is known about the Dutch trade in Asia than anywhere else because the VOC kept meticulous records on the buying and selling of goods. The prices paid in the commodity auctions in Holland were three times higher than their purchase price in Asia.[47] For example, in the 1660s goods from Asia to a value of 31 million guilders were sent to the Netherlands where they netted a profit of 92 million guilders. The scale of the profits changed in the eighteenth century, as the profit margins were reduced, investment costs became higher and the VOC – suffering the effects of paying high dividends of 16.5 per cent – went into debt. Both the VOC shareholders who pocketed the high dividends and the Dutch traders who re-exported the goods from Asia on the European or American markets profited from the trade with Asia. So it was no wonder that leading Amsterdam merchants such as Gerrit Bicker or Gerrit Reynst were involved in trade with both the West and East Indies. The East Indies trade made it possible for many of the VOC's employees to climb the social ladder back in the Netherlands if they had had a career in Asia and had made a fortune – whether legally or illegally.

If one examines the development of Dutch trade as a whole, one cannot fail to see how it expanded enormously in the seventeenth century and to appreciate the supremacy of the

Dutch in international trade. Even though some setbacks occurred towards the end of the seventeenth century, for example in the Mediterranean and Africa, the general picture was extremely stable and this was to continue to characterize the development of trade in the eighteenth century. The Dutch dominated world trade because they were market leaders in trading in mass-produced and luxury goods. The Dutch were able to dominate the luxury goods trade only because their processing industries were technically superior and, in turn, these industries profited from the almost unlimited supplies of dyewoods, chemicals and rare raw materials that the overseas trade was able to secure for them. The only way neighbouring countries could have destroyed the Dutch lead would have been by military means or by subsidizing their merchants.

However, even the trade wars between England and the Netherlands did not manage to undermine Dutch supremacy.[48] Although the First Navigation Act (1651) decreed that goods from abroad had to be imported directly from the exporting country to England and that they could only be transported either on ships belonging to the country of origin or English ships, this had little effect. As long as England was not in a position to play her role as a trade power fully or at least supply her own settlers in the overseas colonies adequately, the Navigation Act could not be put into practice. Thus shortly after the conflict was resolved, Dutch trade had returned to its pre-war level. In the long run, import bans and high import duties imposed by the trading nations on some Dutch products proved to be detrimental, since they ruined the trade in the affected industrial sectors.

Of course the financial sector also contributed to the success of Dutch trade since the merchants provided it with sufficient capital and thus created a further competitive advantage.[49] The most important event in seventeenth-century Dutch financial history was the founding of the Amsterdam Wisselbank in 1609.[50] The Wisselbank succeeded the public deposit and clearing banks that had been established in Italy in the second half of the sixteenth century. The foundation of the Wisselbank stopped the unregulated exchange and lending activities of the private *kassiers* (money-lenders) and transferred them to a public exchange bank.

The Wisselbank quickly became successful and it enjoyed a good reputation both at home and abroad. Further exchange banks were founded in Middelburg (1616), Delft (1621), Rotterdam (1635), and Hamburg (1619). The Wisselbank performed four essential functions for the Dutch economy during the seventeenth century. Out of the monetary chaos of the early seventeenth century it created stable coins, which the Dutch needed as trade coins (*negotienpenningen*) in the Baltic, the Levant and the East Indies. The bank also established an international clearing system for bills of exchange – merchants had an account in the bank on which they could draw bills, and the bank would transfer the amount from one account to another. According to the regulations, all transactions of over six hundred guilders had to be cleared by the bank and, as a result, all the important companies opened accounts which in turn encouraged cashless transactions. The procedure for lending money was less important, since this was against the bank's statutes. However, institutions such as local governments, for example the city of Amsterdam and the VOC, were able to borrow money.

The final important function of the Wisselbank concerned the precious metals trade. From 1683 onwards, bank customers were allowed to deposit precious metals in the bank and their value was credited to the customers' accounts. They were given a receipt (*recepis*) for the precious metals that they had deposited and because they could use these receipts to settle other debts, the merchants left their precious metals in the bank and the bank traded with their customers' gold and silver. Thus Amsterdam became the most important international precious metal market, since it was possible to obtain any Dutch trade coin whatsoever, and extensive amounts of every other large European coin.

Amsterdam's financial position was not determined by the Wisselbank alone: the seventeenth century saw the revival of the private banking institutions, which were still connected with their mercantile function. Merchant-bankers gave acceptance credits, that is, they accepted bills of exchange which their clients could draw on, but it was the client's responsibility to ensure that enough money was in his account on the due date.[51] Thus the bankers not only financed the Amsterdam trade but also a large part of eighteenth-century international trade in London or

Hamburg. The banks also placed state loans which, because of the large amount of money that the population saved, were very well subscribed to, as were the shares in the trading companies.[52] Owning shares – like investing in ships, land reclamation and land improvement – was a phenomenon that was widespread at all levels of society. The *Tulpomania* of the 1630s showed that people were not afraid to take risks or to speculate in commodity futures. The low interest rates offered by the Dutch state loans indicate that large amounts of capital were available. The interest rate fell from 8.33 per cent in 1600 to 6.25 per cent in 1611 and then to 5 per cent in 1640; after 1672 the interest rate fluctuated between 3 and 3.75 per cent. In contrast, the interest on English government bonds was 10 per cent in 1624 and gradually sank to 6 per cent in 1651 and 5 per cent in 1714.[53] It is therefore hardly surprising that the Dutch invested a great deal of money in the English public debt during the eighteenth century, since they could get a much higher return in England. The low capital costs were also extremely advantageous for a business community that stockpiled large amounts of goods and, because the centres of production were very far away, had to accept that the capital which they invested would take a long time to be amortized.[54]

Even after 1670, when both industry and fishing recorded a marked drop in their economic positions and the value of their sales, the financial and trading sectors contributed to the fact that though the performance of the Dutch economy stagnated, it did so at a high level and did not decline dramatically. This serves to explain why the per capita income of the Dutch remained either unaffected by these developments or even slightly increased.

7   Gerard Terborch, *Deventer Magistrates*, 1667, Deventer, Town Hall.

III

Dutch Society

The change from an aristocratic to a bourgeois society that took place in the Netherlands in the seventeenth century, was unique in Europe because Dutch society was dominated by an advanced urban élite. The Dutch no longer defined their social position by enumerating the privileges conferred on them by birth but instead by their mercantile status. Their world was urban in character and was based on non-agrarian activities. Almost half of the population was already living in cities and only a third still worked in agriculture. Since, in spite of the advanced urbanization, at least half of the populace lived in the country, the urban and rural societies are considered separately, beginning with the rural society and the position of the aristocracy, the church and the peasants.

There were relatively few Dutch aristocrats in the early modern European era and their role was limited accordingly. While the aristocracy represented the 'political and socially privileged ruling class' in other European countries,[1] a century and a half of continuous feuding and an above average mortality-rate among the aristocracy had greatly reduced the number of aristocratic Dutch families. In the sixteenth century, there were only twelve aristocratic families left (in the eighteenth century, only seven) and they owned less than ten per cent of the arable land.[2] In Friesland and Groningen no aristocrats enjoyed absolute privileges by virtue of their birth. The only aristocrats in these regions were the *hoofdelingen* who had emerged from the class of prosperous peasants during the Middle Ages and, among their other privileges, lived in fortified houses called *stinzen*. Only in Geldern and Overijssel did aristocrats occupy a more important position. Here the peasants' ties to the land and to the lords of the manor were stronger than in the north and the north-west, where the few aristocrats who had land there generally leased it to the 'free' peasants.

The middle-class environment in the state affairs and politics still resulted in a certain deference to the aristocracy, most of whom lived at the court of the House of Orange in The Hague. As the sole deputy of the country outside the towns and as the 'First (and only) member in the States General, the aristocracy wielded a more extensive influence that one would imagine from its size'.[3] However, the provincial aristocracy's economic position seems to have worsened towards the end of the seventeenth century. The aristocratic landowners who were living off the rents paid by their peasants were particularly badly affected and suffered financial losses. In Overijssel, for example, the aristocracy's share of the province's taxable wealth in 1758 was only nineteen per cent – in 1675 it had still been as high as forty-one per cent. More and more of the land owned by the aristocrats was taken over by city dwellers and especially by the more prosperous peasants such as the *hoofdelingen* who thus increased their land ownership.

Like the aristocracy, the church played only a secondary role as a rural landowner. Solely in the diocese of Utrecht did the cathedral chapter and church foundations have manorial rights. Apart from this, the monasteries, especially in Friesland and Holland, were the largest ecclesiastical landowners. However, this changed in the 1590s when the new provinces confiscated land from the monasteries and proceeded to administer it themselves.[4] Once this had happened, the revenue from these estates was used to maintain village schools, newly founded universities, hospitals and orphanages. The increase in the amount of land owned by the cities became particularly significant, gradually exceeding that owned by the aristocracy and the church. If the cities had originally expanded into the surrounding countryside in order to secure an economic hinterland to support the urban economy, in the course of the seventeenth century more and more middle-class capital flowed into the rural areas as people bought land and invested in land reclamation projects. People from the cities often worked on these projects with the peasants who were the social group most affected by the dynamic expansion of rural society.

The agricultural economy was firmly based on the right of ownership. In the province of Holland, for example, the peasants owned more than forty per cent of the land themselves. They could use their land and its produce as they pleased, without being forced to submit to pressure from the lords of the manor, and this, along with the favourable agrarian economy, triggered the introduction of a more intensive type of agriculture. Dutch agriculture was subject to the laws of the market economy: 'Some peasants owned much land, leased it to other peasants, lent money, and engaged in local trade. Other peasants owned nothing and found themselves economically dependent not upon noblemen, churchmen, or their representatives, but upon other peasants.'[5] The grain imported from the Baltic area freed both the resources of the land and the workers for other productive, high-yielding agricultural sectors. Peasants were particularly interested in animal husbandry and in producing butter and cheese; they specialized in cultivating industrial crops such as madder for export.[6]

Peasants spared no expense in reclaiming land or in mechanizing their businesses. These investments and the resultant increase in productivity paid off, particularly in the seventeenth century when the great majority of European peasants had to cope with the increasing agrarian depression.[7] As agriculture became more specialized, so did the division of labour and the social differentiation among the rural population. Peasants employed other rural workers for many jobs so that they could keep their own workers exclusively for their own more profitable enterprises. As well as their farm-hands, they employed day-labourers to build and maintain sluice gates and dykes, and to dig turf. Numerous craftsmen as well as wagon drivers and skippers who had a whole range of services to offer settled in the villages. Thus the traditional farming class split into a class of rich peasants on the one hand and a rural labouring class on the other. The long-term result of these changes was that the class that was made up of the rural labourers and the craftsmen grew more quickly than the peasants, even though the members of this rural lower class regularly migrated to the cities.

However, owing to the high wages, working on the land was considered to be a very attractive proposition throughout the seventeenth century.[8] A day-labourer received fifteen to twenty stuivers a day, which approaches that of the craftsmen's journeymen in the city who, by 1650, were usually getting twenty stuivers. Just as interesting is the fact that rural wages were still rising in the second half of the seventeenth century, while urban wages had already begun to stagnate. Numerous contemporary accounts mention these high wages. In 1662 the politician Pieter de la Court complained that 'the farmers must pay such high salaries and day wages to their servants that they live with great difficulty, while their servants are very comfortable. The same discomfort is felt by men in the cities, where the craftsmen and servants are more unbearable than in any other land.'[9] The peasants also tried to reduce their wage bill by mechanizing their business and using seasonal workers. For example, in dairy farming they used a butter churn (the *karnemolen*), powered by horses, which replaced many milkmaids. Towards the end of the seventeenth century, Dutch peasants preferred to employ seasonal workers from Westphalia, especially at harvest time.

What were rural incomes like? Only general tendencies can be sketched owing to the lack of sources. A rural worker in the seventeenth century earnt more than an independent peasant a century earlier. On the other hand, the peasants had profited both from the increase in the agricultural prices and the profitability of the land that was reflected in the rising rents. The probate inventories compiled by Jan de Vries provide a fairly accurate picture of the peasants' level of prosperity and the material goods that they owned.[10] While the sixteenth-century farmhouses rarely had more items of furniture than two tables and usually had fewer than ten chairs, this had changed by the seventeenth century. Large oak chests, octagonal tables, curtains and carpets all became more common. The most expensive current items of furniture were the beds; these were viewed by contemporaries as status symbols and the number of beds reflected the wealth of peasants' households. However, peasants demonstrated their prosperity to the outside world by their gold and silver buckles, buttons, beakers and spoons. The peasant Cornelius Pieterse de Lange who died in Alphen in 1692 left rings, jewellery, three earrings, four spoons and various hair pins. To put this in perspective, the cost of four silver spoons could have provided one person with enough bread for a year. Apart from this, the probate inventories prove that the tales of Dutch peasants who bought paintings were true. Cornelius Jacob Maals, another peasant who also died in Alphen in 1692, owned sixteen paintings, a mirror, an octagonal table and curtains, as well as various decorative glazed tiles.

However, most of the peasants left few paintings and several never owned any. They tended to own more textiles: 'The average farmer of seventeenth-century Friesland could choose each morning from over a dozen shirts while, in the mid-seventeenth century, his linen chests were laden with nearly 40 bedsheets, 4 handcloths, 6 tablecloths, and a dozen table napkins.'[11] Apart from this, considerable cash legacies from 290–310 guilders, government bonds and promissory notes indicate the considerable financial resources in the villages.[12] Wealth and income were – next to family relationships and education – the most important criteria for measuring social status in urban Dutch society. Those who lived in the cities in early modern times had a great deal of respect for possessions. Regents were classified according to the size of their fortune, and the bankrupt, 'who had gambled away his own fortune and those of others'[13] was despised. For example, the *Verenigde Oost-Indische Compagnie* (VOC) was expressly forbidden to employ bankrupts, Catholics or people with a bad reputation in their Asian trade.

In contrast to the lack of information about the rural areas there are numerous studies about Dutch urban society. In the seventeenth century, people even tried to consolidate their place in the urban society by defining the social hierarchy. Historians have studied these records in recent times and applied sociological models to the historical descriptions of the different social groups. An initial model of society based on class was drawn up by Renier in 1948, with aristocrats, a bourgeoisie, a broad middle class, a middle class and a lower class.[14] This was replaced by Roorda's analysis of Holland and Zeeland, in which he divided the society into five classes:[15]

(1) the patriciate – Regents, leading merchants and large manufacturers
(2) the broad middle class – prosperous merchants, traders and academics
(3) the middle class – traders and skilled craftsmen

(4) the lower class made up of workers and servants
(5) the *grauw*, the rabble.

Roorda's model has since been further refined by Gerrit
Groenhuis, who also took marriage patterns (*l'intermarriage*) and
wealth into account as an indication of people's status. Groenhuis
divided society into six classes and included the rural population,
which is not really of interest here:[16]

(1) aristocrats and Regents
(2) rich merchants, large ship owners, businessmen, some of
    the doctors, incumbents of high offices, directors of trad-
    ing companies, high-ranking officers who do not belong to
    the Regents' families
(3) larger traders, master craftsmen, skippers with at least a
    medium-sized ship, lower-ranking officers, those holding
    official offices (municipal doctor, rector etc.)
(4) less important bureaucrats, clerks, small traders, craftsmen,
    skippers and the self-employed
(5) workers receiving wages (porters), seamen/sailors, sol-
    diers, lightermen, millhands, and other labourers
(6) vagrants, beggars, invalids, discharged soldiers and sailors,
    migrant workers, actors.

A contemporary description by the Amsterdam broker Joris
Craffurd in 1686 tends to support Groenhuis' divisions:

to put it this way, there are many different types of people: The
first are the men in government, those who are dependent on
them and those who are moving up into the government. The
second are the numerous very distinguished, impressive, rich
merchants. The third are traders or shop owners including
many master craftsmen and craftsmen. The fourth are the
ranks by which we mean the lowest sort of people, however, we
should exclude the numerous wagon drivers, grain porters,
lightermen, peat and beer porters all of whom receive alms
which does not often make them the most respectful and civi-
lized people.[17]

However, it should be borne in mind that this slightly derogatory
verdict was given by someone who was on the second highest rung

of the social ladder and whose view became more jaundiced the lower he looked.

What was life really like for these different social classes? Owing to the difficulty of finding trustworthy sources, more is known about some social groups than others. The urban governing class, the Regents, is, for example, well documented. By the seventeenth century, this small group of approximately two thousand people had developed into an exclusive élite, which divided the state and municipal offices between them. In the cities this meant the mayoralties, membership of the city council and the office of Post Master, as well as a few lesser positions. At the provincial and republican level, these offices ranged from posts in the States General and the provincial and municipal governments (*regerings collegies*) to the office of the Grand Pensionary (*raadpensionaris*). The offices were divided using contracts (*contracten van correspondentie*), that the Regent families concluded between themselves and which regulated the distribution of the lucrative offices thus avoiding disputes between the different families.

Although many offices were inherited by certain families in the seventeenth century , the Regent class was not hermetically sealed from the rest of society. It was still possible for families to be accepted into the circle of the Regents.[18] Some Regent families were much richer than others, in Amsterdam you naturally had to have many more possessions or greater wealth to be admitted to the Regent class than in smaller cities such as Leeuwarden or Harlingen, where small merchants who were less prosperous could become Regents. This difference in wealth between Leeuwarden and Amsterdam in the middle of the seventeenth century can be seen by looking at the records: in 1672, 271 people in Leeuwarden had a fortune of over 10,000 guilders (the average was 33,359 guilders); in 1674, 259 people in Amsterdam had fortunes of 100,000 guilders or more.

Joop Faber has compiled a picture of Harlingen based on its citizens' wealth.[19] The first group (with a fortune of 20,000–50,000 guilders) contained a senior official of the admiralty, two merchants and a wood merchant, the second group (10,000–19,000 guilders) was composed of men of private means and merchants. In the third group (4,000–9,000 guilders) there were, among others, an ensign of the urban militia and two pastors, one of them a military chaplain. Among those on the fourth level (1,000–3,900 guilders) were two former mayors, a rector, a miller, an apothecary, a clerk in the lending house, a button maker, a municipal surgeon, and a dyer. The penultimate group (100–900 guilders) was made up of small skippers, a cooper, a tailor and other craftsmen. In the sixth and lowest group were those without any wealth, such as porters, apprentices, sailors and soldiers, but he also found a schoolmaster and a deputy headmaster.

People's wealth was, of course, related to the size of their income which, the higher one climbed up the monetary ladder, came from increasingly varied sources. To take the Regents as an example: the money that they received for carrying out their duties was only a small part of their income when compared with the indirect profit from the office itself, or their income from trade and capital investments. Nevertheless, the Grand Pensionary Johan de Witt received three thousand guilders annually when he was appointed to a five-year term of office.[20] At this time an average worker could have earned only about a tenth of that amount.[21] However, in the first half of the seventeenth century wages rose, and they remained stable in the second half of the century. Since prices fell after 1665, the purchasing power of the working population increased. Even the group earning the lowest wages profited from this phenomenon as long as they were not affected by unemployment, illness or invalidity. Porters, millhands, sailors, boom keepers and schoolmasters with an annual income of 150 guilders lived on the edge of, or even under, subsistence level depending on whether or not they had families. Women and children had to work as well and were in demand as textile industry workers.

However, it must be stressed that the wages paid in Dutch cities and in rural areas were the highest in Europe. This led to continual economic immigration, especially to Amsterdam which was a flourishing trade and service centre. This urban development can be seen clearly in the Amsterdam marriage register which noted the place of birth of the bride and bridegroom.[22] Throughout the seventeenth century, the majority of men who married there had not only been born outside the city, but even outside Holland itself. At the beginning of the century most of

them came from Flanders, later on many came from Germany
and even from Scandinavia. One of the great paradoxes of this
economic development was that while the Dutch job market
remained attractive to foreign workers – even when it was only
seasonal work – members of the Dutch lower class were only a
small step away from unemployment and a gradual decline into
becoming part of the marginal group known as the *grauw*. This
meant living off other people's charity, above all that of church
institutions and the numerous charitable foundations which
existed in the Netherlands during the Golden Age. Jan de Vries
has suggested that, in view of the demand for workers and the
shortage of workers in certain sectors, and the continual immigration of workers, unemployment was also a consciously chosen
leisure time, which was facilitated by the activities of the charitable
institutions.[23] The municipal policy for the poor took as its starting point the fiction that the beggars were really looking for work
and they should be helped to do so. This finally led to the beggars
being compulsorily included in the working process by the
municipal workhouses.[24] However, it was clear to many contemporaries that even the beggars were following a sort of profession,
which was based on training as well as experience. For example,
Adriaen van de Venne described forty-two different types of
tramps and beggars, each with its special system of begging. When
compared with Europe as a whole however, begging in the
Netherlands did not seem to have increased substantially; foreign
visitors to the country commented on the uncommonly small
number of beggars and they were astounded that people were
able to travel safely there, even at night.[25]

Owing to this unemployment and begging, which presumably
got worse at the end of the seventeenth century, one could mistak-
enly think that the people's material situation worsened dramatically during this period. It has already been shown that the wage
earners' buying power had increased due to the fall in prices, and
that the Dutch per capita income also increased throughout the
seventeenth century. Its rise, even at the end of the century, was
calculated by the English mathematician and statistician Gregory
King who estimated the Dutch per capita income in 1695 to be £8
2s 9d (approx. 100 guilders) and stressed that it continued to

grow.[26] This means that the Dutch per capita income was unquestionably the highest in Europe.

The rate at which private wealth grew tends to support the premise that the per capita income had increased. In 1585, 65 Amsterdam households (out of about 30,000 inhabitants) had taxable wealth of 10,000 guilders or more. Only ninety years later in 1674, 259 households (out of 200,000 inhabitants) had 100,000 guilders or more; in these circles 10,000 guilders was not worth talking about.[27] By 1680, in the medium-sized city of Gouda where you would be counted as on of the city's richer citizens if you had 10,000 guilders, fortunes of over 10,000 guilders had increased five-fold since 1599.[28] This development continued until the eighteenth century, by which time a considerable amount of the wealth that had been accumulated came from capital returns – but the precise details of this have not been calculated. Capital investors were considered to be members of the middle class, which, because of its high level of savings, regularly invested money in state and provincial loans or in shares in the trading companies thus increasing their wealth in the long term. It is important to remember that, in this society, people who accumulated wealth were able to advance socially.

How was social mobility organized in Dutch society during the seventeenth century? On the one hand, people were expected to know their place and to seek their social contacts and spouses from among their own class; on the other, Calvinism viewed professional success positively, it propounded the philosophy of *carrière ouverte au caractère*.[29] In practice, the middle class, that is, the third and fourth groups in Groenhuis' model, had the best chance of advancing socially and they could do this in several stages – it was even possible for them to become members of the Regents' patriciate.

Even when in the course of the seventeenth century, the members of the Regent class increasingly isolated themselves from other classes, the studies of Amsterdam and Zierikzee show that it was still possible to advance socially.[30] The political crises in 1618/19 and 1672 brought new blood into the city government and new parties came to power without changing the fundamental political and social structures. People who wanted to advance socially could also move to Amsterdam which, as the *entrepôt* of the world, attracted potential social climbers from both inside and outside the country. Elias Trip, who was born in Zaltbommel in 1570 and died in Amsterdam in 1636, is a good example of this kind of successful mercantile career.[31] Together with his brother Jacob (1576–1661) he settled in Dordrecht; his main trade was in iron, but he was also involved in other enterprises. Soon Dordrecht became too small for the ambitious merchant so he moved to Amsterdam. Here Trip dealt successfully in weapons and in its contingent trade – Swedish copper. In the first half of the seventeenth century, the Netherlands was the centre of the European weapons trade. In 1631, just fifteen years after his move to Amsterdam, Elias Trip, with his fortune of 240,000 guilders, had become one of Amsterdam's twenty-four richest citizens.

The trading ethos of the Amsterdam élite was kept alive by the continuous migration of merchants and the rise of these new men into the city's ruling class. When a family became aristocratic and retired from trading, new trading families took its place.[32] It was only after 1680, when Amsterdam to all intents and purposes stopped expanding, that the *rentier* (gentleman of leisure) mentality gained ground. This, the highest form of advancement (from trader to gentleman of leisure and professional politician who was able to live off the income generated by his capital), happened in the Amsterdam Regent class. For example, people were more likely to be told about the Regents' country houses than about their professions.[33]

The change in lifestyle that accompanied such advancement can be seen by looking at several generations of one of these families such as the de Graeffs. Dirck Graeff, who became Mayor of Amsterdam in 1578, was actively involved in the iron trade. His son, Jacob, also worked as a merchant but he bought the Zuidpolsbroek estate and ennobled himself, becoming Jacob de Graeff, Baron of Zuidpolsbroek. Two of his sons Andries and Cornelis de Graeff were politicians and *rentiers* and, extrapolating from their portraits, Cornelis de Graeff and his wife were quite happy to openly demonstrate their more elevated status.[34]

Social advancement was based on wealth and this could be accumulated in a relatively short space of time in seventeenth-century Amsterdam. The zenith of social advancement however, was reached by marrying into a family that was higher up the

8   Nicolaes Eliasz., known as Pickenoy, *Cornelis de Graeff*, c. 1645,
Berlin Gemäldegalerie in the Bodemuseum Staatliche Museen
Preußischer Kulturbesitz. (Photo: J. P. Anders)

9   Nicolaes Eliasz., known as Pickenoy, *Catherine Hooft* (wife of the politician Cornelis de Graeff, depicted in fig. 8), c. 1645, Berlin, Gemäldegalerie in the Bodemuseum Staatliche Museen Preußischer Kulturbesitz. (Photo: J. P. Anders)

social ladder. If there was not enough money for the lower and middle class to fund their advancement then the only avenues open to them were the navy, serving overseas, or art. The majority of naval officers came from the lower class and this is where many of the most spectacular careers are found, since sailors could rise to the rank of admiral. This was what the Dutch maritime heroes Pieter Pietersz. Heyn, Maarten Harpertsz. Tromp and Michael Adriaensz. de Ruyter did, all of whom had begun as simple sailors or even as ship's boys. In the late seventeenth century however, the captains and those making a career in the overseas branches of trading companies, came from the middle if not the upper classes. Jan Pietersz. Coen, who founded Dutch trading power in South East Asia, was the son of a fishmonger from Twist, near Hoorn. However, young Coen's father sent him to Italy to learn double-entry bookkeeping, thus enabling him to rise from being a bookkeeper for the VOC to being its most successful Governor General. Coen's career also demonstrates that education or training was becoming increasingly important as a tool of social advancement. The Director General of the WIC, Pieter Stuyvesant, who was a pastor's son and had married a pastor's daughter, came from the educated middle class.

Finally, the artistic careers that are considered in some detail elsewhere in this book should be mentioned. Rembrandt was the son of a miller and the grandson of a baker – both from Leiden, and attended the Latin school and later Leiden University. After his artistic training and work as a free master in Leiden, in 1631 he moved to Amsterdam where he crowned his artistic career by marrying Saskia van Uylenburgh, the daughter of the Mayor of Leeuwarden. Rembrandt's pupils – Ferdinand Bol, who, after marrying a rich widow, ended his life as the Regent of a charitable foundation living in a house in the upper-class Keizersgracht in Amsterdam, and the highly paid 'Painter Prince' Gerrit van Honthorst from Utrecht, who was able to afford the ultimate status symbol of the rich: a coach – were less prominent but no less successful. When painters were artistically and financially success-ful, they quickly became accustomed to the lifestyle of their mid-dle-class or aristocratic clients. They bought houses in exclusive areas, filled their studios with works of art by foreign masters, precious objects and curiosities (which were meant to underline their social position) even when they, like Rembrandt, could not always afford them.

Dutch society possessed a wide variety of status symbols which were subtly displayed behind a façade of apparent simplicity. They ranged from clothing, horses and coaches to houses and furnishing, and from seating arrangements and precedence at celebrations and in churches, to the bearing of titles.[35] Thus, although people dressed discreetly in black, which gives the present-day viewer an impression of restraint, the material was so fine, and was trimmed with such expensive lace that everyone was perfectly aware of just how prosperous they were. Like today, the upper class avidly followed Parisian fashions in clothing and hairstyles. For example, the wearing of wigs was no longer restricted to the patriciate. The middle class dressed more modestly because the Parisian fashions were expensive; a pair of good French stockings, for example, cost fourteen guilders, a sum that could keep someone in bread for six months. The Rolls-Royce of the seventeenth century was a barouche drawn by two horses. The Gouda Regent Frans Herbert was considered to be a social climber, and was described somewhat dismissively as someone who 'used to be a modest person but, since he has begun travelling in a horse-drawn barouche, has arrogance shining from his eyes.'[36]

House furnishings and the paintings that were hung in the home all proclaimed their owner's social standing. Porcelain, tapestries, furniture and pictures demonstrated not only upper-class prosperity, middle-class households were remarkable for the tastefulness of their household possessions as well. The middle class also had family or individual portraits painted, and painters benefited from the fact that this particular status symbol was no longer restricted to the patriciate and the upper class. The church pew was another status symbol and more and more groups demanded their own seats. In the Stevenskerk in Nijmegen, for example, a new pew was erected for the members of the council in 1644; this led to the officers of the garrison and the aristocrats living in the town having their own pews, a trend that was, in turn, followed by the lawyers and the doctors. In 1662, the riding masters and the captains were allocated their own pew, followed, two years later, by the educated children of the Regents and finally, in 1669, certain people whom the Mayor deemed worthy were given their own pew. Thus the social advancement of the middle class resulted in a fight over the allocation of church pews![37]

The final status symbol that will mentioned here is godparents. They were carefully chosen by the child's parents and they usually had the same status as the parents of the child to be baptized, or sometimes higher. One could be forgiven for thinking that the parents went to a lot of trouble to gather as illustrious an assembly as possible around the font. If they fell a little short on the illustrious stakes then the next best thing was to ensure a large number of godparents.

In all, seventeenth-century Dutch society seems to be unique in early modern Europe. Its political and social life was not dominated by a king, the aristocracy or the church, but by those belonging to the Regent class and the urban upper class, that is, the burghers or the bourgeoisie. In France, for example, this group, the *tiers état*, came to power only with the French Revolution. In contrast the Dutch middle class already had political power in the smaller and medium-sized towns. This prosperous middle class, together with the rich peasants, stimulated much of the country's economic, social and artistic development. They constituted not only a pool of well-educated office holders but also represented a growing market for both domestic and foreign commercial and artistic creativity. Also, their willingness to spend money as the upper class did resulted in a socially acceptable economic development in the Netherlands. Numerous charitable establishments such as poor boxes and soup kitchens owed their existence to these prosperous citizens. The result of this extensive social network – even if it was loosely organized – was that no one was forced to starve in the Netherlands even when the health of the poor was weakened owing to a long-term increase in the price of grain.[38]

Despite this rudimentary social security system, the Netherlands was not free from unrest in the seventeenth and eighteenth centuries. However, the upheavals in the Netherlands were markedly different from the rebellions and revolts that had previously taken place in Europe. Dutch unrest was a uniquely urban phenomenon. Rural revolts that occured in France and Central Europe did not take place in the Netherlands at all.[39] Apart from the politically- or religiously-motivated unrest in the years 1617–19,

1653 and 1672, the only other revolts that took place in the Netherlands were those over the price of bread and taxes.

The unrest from 1617 to 1619, which nearly ended in a civil war, flared up over a dispute between two theologians from Leiden, Arminius and Gomarus, about the doctrine of predestination. This acrimonious dispute developed out of an internal university disagreement between the Remonstrants (Arminians) and the Counter-Remonstrants (Gomarians). The Grand Pensionary Johan van Oldenbarnvelt, intervened on the Remonstrant side and the governor (stadholder*), Prince Maurice of Orange, intervened on the opposing side.[40] The dispute ended with Oldenbarnvelt being hanged and his fellow protester Hugo Grotius, the famous lawyer and author, being incarcerated, and resulted in the power of the governor and the military commander being strengthened in comparison with that of the Regents. Even the unrest in 1653 and 1672 was somewhat unusual, owing to the fact that the members of the House of Orange used the lower classes and, in particular, their potential for violence for their own political ends, against the Regent class.[41] Following a twenty-two-year period without a governor, the 1672 revolt led to Wilhelm III being elected as governor. It should also be acknowledged that foreign political events such as Oldenbarnvelt's French policy (1617–19), the outbreak of the First Anglo-Dutch War (1652), and the English defeat of the Dutch in the Third Anglo-Dutch War (1672) played quite an important role in triggering these events.

The tax and bread price revolts that took place in the Netherlands from time to time are, from a social historian's viewpoint, more interesting. In general the tax protests were staged by the middle classes and the bread revolts by the lower classes. However, protests against increases in food prices in 1630 and 1698, as well as in 1693 and 1699, are known to have been caused by the price of butter – not by the price of bread.[42] These were in fact spontaneous protests by the lower classes, including the *grauw*, against small merchants, bakers and the peasants who had come to

---

* The title 'stadholder', literally viceroy to the king of Spain, survived Dutch independence.

market and who were attacked because of their prices, since the increase had the greatest effect on the living standards of the lower classes.

Those involved in the tax protests, however, ranged from individual representatives of the upper class, through to the middle and lower classes.[43] In the early modern period, the Netherlands had a comparatively fair tax system. The tax burden was not exclusively borne by the peasants as was the case in the neighbouring countries, nor were certain social groups exempt from paying tax, which would have increased the burden on other social groups. The main tax burden was borne by the consumer, as an excise duty was levied on all the basic consumer goods – grain, beer, butter, salt, soap, candles, coal, shoes, turf, and animals that were to be slaughtered.[44] Accordingly, practically every time a new form of indirect taxation was introduced or an existing indirect tax was increased, protests arose, some of which were violent, and were often visited on the tax collectors who came from the artisan milieu. When the unrest escalated, the protesters also turned on the authorities who were responsible for increasing the burden.

Although most of the protests were caused by duties on butter, beer and turf, in 1696 there were also demonstrations by the Amsterdam undertakers, the *ansprekersoproer*, which today might be found rather bizarre.[45] The revolt was triggered by the action of an undertaker who was protesting against the establishment of a public burial service. Simultaneously, the public had begun to dispute a new provincial tax levied on weddings and funerals. The rumour began to circulate that although the poor would not have to pay this tax, they would be buried like beggars in a white box with the town crest on it. Those people who had saved for a long time in order to be able to have a respectable burial, found this insulting. On 30 January 1696, a mock burial was arranged on the Dam in front of the Amsterdam town hall. Twenty-four hours later riots began and the houses of those who were presumed to be responsible for introducing the tax were looted. The city authorities felt compelled to act and some of the looters were arrested.

Both the bread and the tax revolts were defensive in nature since the participants expressly referred back to old rights which they were trying to protect. As a rule, they were not very successful because the politicians responsible did not revise their decisions and, even if they had wanted to, would not have been able to do so owing to the parlous state of the budget.[46] As well as this, the towns could use the city militia to repress most revolts quickly and without bloodshed. This meant that the number of people who lost their lives in unrest in the Netherlands during the seventeenth and eighteenth centuries could be counted on the fingers of one hand.[47]

IV

Artists' Origins and their Social Status

When the literary historian Gerard Brom said that 'Painting was a job, writing poetry a hobby',[1] he was describing the very different roles played by the painter and writer in Dutch society. While the painter was able to make a living from his craft, the majority of writers belonged to the upper class and had to subsidize their writing, which was not very profitable, by working as merchants, politicians or diplomats.

This chapter concerns painting as a profession: the painters' origins, how they were educated, how they organized their artistic output and how they were thus able to make a living. Thanks to Michael Montias's seminal study of the artists and craftsmen who lived in Delft, there is a reasonably accurate and complete picture of these painters.[2] Painters' lives were governed by relatively uniform rules under the auspices of the artists' guilds – the Guilds of St Luke – thus what is known about the painters in Delft can be used to form a national picture. However, the famous painters whose origin, education and professional development are better known than the general run of painters present a problem: it is not known how representative their lives are for Dutch painters in general. Owing to this, the conclusions here are based on the statistically verifiable data from regional studies and illustrated by the lives of certain artists.

Most artists came from the province of Holland: from Amsterdam, Rotterdam, Haarlem, Leiden and Delft and from Utrecht, which was also an important artistic centre. However, a painter did not have to remain in the city where he was born and grew up, where he had trained or taken his first independent professional steps. Successful painters often found that their home towns became too restricting and they then, like the Delft painters Simon de Vlieger, Willem van Aelst, Paulus Potter or Pieter de Hooch, went to Amsterdam where there was a larger market for their work. Many painters stopped off in The Hague on their way to Amsterdam because this was where the court of the House of Orange and the States General encouraged the demand for works of art. However, it would be incorrect to think that all painters travelled and some, like Johannes Vermeer, remained in their home towns; during the seventeenth century, the number of painters born in Delft who stayed and practised their craft there continued to increase.[3] The migrants from the southern Netherlands, Flanders and Brabant should also be mentioned. These first or second generation migrants were very strongly represented in the Guild of St Luke and had a considerable influence on the Mannerist style which developed throughout the Netherlands at the beginning of the seventeenth century – for example, Karel van Manders's school in Haarlem, which produced Frans Hals.

The Dutch painter's social origin is even more interesting than his birthplace. Dutch painters were generally thought to have come from the lower social classes[4] and more can be found out about their social backgrounds by looking at what their fathers or guardians did. For example, twenty-six of the sixty-seven Delft painters whose origins are known about and who were registered with the guild between 1613 and 1679, were the sons or wards of painters, art dealers, engravers or glass-makers who were themselves members of the Guild of St Luke in Delft or elsewhere.[5] The fathers of nine of them were goldsmiths, silversmiths or jewellers, eleven others were craftsmen, eleven more were self-employed, one was a landlord, and nine were wealthy citizens, among them brewers and merchants who accounted for almost a third of the painters. It is also worth mentioning that the number of painters whose fathers were painters fell during the seventeenth century. Montias deduced from this that a talent for painting was possibly becoming more important than the family's artisan tradition.

Based on their fathers' professions, it can be seen that, as a general rule, the painters' backgrounds were solidly middle class. Neither textile workers and skippers nor even the masters of the Delft faïenciers allowed their sons to become painters. The Haarlem painters followed the same pattern: among thirteen

painters born between 1575 and 1600 who have been studied, six
came from painter's families, three from craftsmen's families and
from the self-employed, four from the class comprizing small
craftsmen and workers, and one from the upper class.[6] The fact
that the fathers or the guardians were not exactly the poorest of
Dutch citizens probably reflects the amount of money that
parents had to pay for their sons' artistic education.

Details of the costs and the type of education and training that
artists received during the usual six-year apprenticeship can be
found by looking at the apprenticeship contracts that have survived and which were agreed between the master and the apprentice's father or guardian. Two of these apprenticeship contracts
are examined here in some detail. Firstly the one-year apprenticeship contract between the still life painter Cornelis Jacobsz. Delff
and the guardians of Jan Jansz. van Waterwijk, which was signed
on 1 April 1620. Delff promised to provide the young man with
board and lodging and 'to instruct him in all that concerns the art
and science of painting'[7]; everything that Jan Jansz. painted would
belong to his master. The master received 18 Flemish pounds
(108 guilders) payable in two instalments and this is all that is
known about Jan Jansz. van Waterwijk's career. His father, who
had died in 1619, was a wealthy wine merchant whose estate
brought in almost 2,000 guilders when it was realized. Secondly
the set of apprenticeship contracts that the master glass-maker
Cornelis Ariensz. van Linschoten concluded with the flower
painter Joris Gerritsz. van Lier, dated 1623, are studied. Van Lier
agreed to accept van Linschoten's son, Adriaen Cornelisz.
Linschoten, who was then aged about fifteen or sixteen, as an
apprentice and undertook to give him board and lodging and to
instruct him in the art of painting. As in the contract previously
mentioned, the apprentice's work belonged to the master, who
also received 18 Flemish pounds, but this time it covered a two-
year period.

The fact that van Lier's training was only half as expensive as
Delff's may be due to Delff's reputation: he had been a member
of the guild for many years as a painter of fruit and vegetable still
lifes as well as of domestic scenes; whereas van Lier became a
member of the guild only the day after he signed the apprenticeship contracts. Nevertheless, more is known about Adriaen

Cornelisz. Linschoten's career. When he finished his apprenticeship he went to Italy, and, on returning to the Netherlands in 1635 he became a member of the Delft Guild of St Luke. In the 1650s he moved to The Hague where he was a successful painter.

Finishing an artistic education by travelling to Italy was the exception rather than the rule for Dutch painters – except for those from Utrecht, more than a quarter of whom visited Italy and were known as the Utrecht Caravaggists.[8] Most parents could not afford to send their sons either to France or Italy to complete their education, whereas the education and training available in the Netherlands with a respected master was affordable. Studying at home also had the advantage of ensuring that, by choosing his teacher carefully, the prospective painter could become part of the well-paid artistic community.

The apprenticeship contracts demonstrate that the costs of this education differed widely, depending on the teacher's reputation, how old the pupil was, and whether or not board and lodging in the teacher's house was included. When the master retained rights to the apprentice's paintings – as was usually the case – that reduced the cost, and was why the apprentice was not allowed to sign his work. On average, the annual premium was between twenty and fifty guilders for an apprentice who lived with his parents and between fifty and one hundred guilders for someone who had board and lodging in his master's house. Some pupils, however, paid up to one hundred guilders per annum (without board and lodging) to be taught by the famous teachers such as Honthorst, Rembrandt or Dou.[9] This was an extremely expensive option for the pupil's parents, who also had to feed and clothe their children. Parents who allowed their sons to become painters had to be prepared for a long financially lean period, after a school education that in general cost only about two to six guilders a year they then had to pay about one hundred guilders annually for the painting apprenticeship over a period of six years when the apprentice lived in his master's house. Apart from all this, the parents also had to do without their son's potential earnings as long as he was being trained, but since the fathers were often master-craftsmen they seemed to be able to afford the expense.[10] A prospective painter who did not come from a well-situated family would have had to have overcome almost insuperable obstacles: the fact that the Delft orphanage did not allow any of its charges to be educated as either painters or silversmiths serves to underline this.

What was the apprentice's training really like? In the first part of the seventeenth century, emphasis was placed on the practical aspects. At the end of the sixteenth century, Karel van Mander wanted to introduce new standards for the education of young Dutch painters in his set of instructions for young painters, but this showed how little he understood of the social conditions which prevailed in the Netherlands and governed Dutch paint-ing.[11] Proceeding from the premise of a 'noble, free art', he propagated the Italian or Flemish ideal of the free artist who was principally interested in choosing a renowned master to study with. The Dutch apprenticeship system did not leave much room for such Renaissance niceties. The masters tried to increase their incomes by training the apprentices and by retaining the rights to their work, despite the fact that the apprentice premiums were controlled by the guilds. The apprentices were generally satisfied with their training since, naturally, they remained unaware of the possibility of a theoretical instruction. Their education was there-fore limited to reproducing the master's works. Lessons basically consisted of the apprentice copying a 'correct' version and com-paring the copy with the original. Accordingly, the master's speci-ality whether it was still lifes, genre pictures or seascapes, influenced the pupil's later choice of subject-matter.[12] If the mas-ter did not have many apprentices in his painting school then the tie between the master and pupil was very close. The pupil was son, apprentice and slave all in one. He lived in his master's household, laboured and, when he did not obey, was physically punished.

The framework of the education received by the apprentices was defined in the statutes of the Guild of St Luke, which also ensured that a master could not benefit from an apprentice's education to the detriment of other masters. This led to a limita-tion on the number of apprentices, but it was difficult to ensure that this condition was observed. Perhaps both the masters and apprentices were encouraged to place the apprenticeship con-tracts before the heads of the guild – the eldermen – so that they could be checked.

The guilds were also involved in assessing whether the apprentices' education had been successful.[13] If an apprentice could convince them that he had worked to his master's satisfaction he could hope to have his apprenticeship shortened and to be allowed to undertake his own further education as a journeyman. At the beginning of the apprenticeship however, a certain level of control was necessary. The apprenticeship contracts had a two-month trial period built into them, which the apprentice did not have to pay for. The master was obliged to pay only one guilder into the guild's coffers for each apprentice after the end of this trial period. After two years, apprentices themselves paid the guild two to four stuivers.

The guild had very little control over the quality of the individual apprentice's education because, in general, it followed a traditional pattern.[14] During the first year, the apprentice generally carried out labouring work and acquired the basic craft skills associated with painting. He ground colours, stretched canvases and cleaned brushes and palettes. Then he began his first drawing lessons. Michiel Sweerts's painting (fig. 10) shows how the apprentices drew from engravings, plaster models, anatomic figures, and later from live models. This was followed by studying and then painting clothing. The pupils copied the pictures by their teachers and other masters, and then painted from plaster and live models. In the final phase of their education, they painted the same subjects as their masters, thus they were trained to follow their master's compositional pattern. The fact that the apprentices worked on the same themes made it easier for the masters to correct them, because the apprentices' strengths and weaknesses were then more obvious.

When the master and the head of the Guild of St Luke were satisfied with an apprentice's work, the apprenticeship was ended and the pupil achieved the status of a journeyman. A journeyman was allowed to sign and sell his own pictures and he could work towards becoming a master in the guild. Journeymen often increased their skill even more by working in studios belonging to other masters. At the same time, the practice of employing more journeymen in the bigger studios led to a large-scale division of labour and to art being mass produced. For example, in the case of Michiel van Miereveld's portraits, his sons, grandsons and journeymen worked on them. The portraits of the members of the court of the House of Orange were done by journeymen and were stockpiled against future demand. Miereveld just signed them, sometimes reworking them with one or two brushstrokes. The fact that some of his work was signed 'painted by myself' (*door mij zelven geschilded*) may indicate that – like other artists – he differentiated between his own work and that produced by his studio, a difference that would have been reflected in the price.

The professional career of Dutch painters was, like their artistic output, governed by regulations laid down by the Guild of St Luke. A pupil joined the Guild of St Luke in the third year of his apprenticeship and hoped, some time after the end of the apprenticeship, to be accepted in the guild as a master; then, as a rule, he would remain in the guild until his death, when the guild members would be obliged to pay their last respects at his funeral.

The Guild of St Luke dated from the Middle Ages and was a corporation of artists and craftsmen. It was named after Luke the Evangelist who, according to legend, lived in Antioch where he worked as a painter and a doctor, he is thought to have painted the first picture of the Madonna. The Reformation in the northern part of the Netherlands did not affect St Luke's patronage of the guild, even though by then the guild had become secular in character and had experienced a revival at the end of the sixteenth and the beginning of the seventeenth century as a craft guild. In Amsterdam in 1579 'the painters, glass makers, carvers, carvers of figures, embroiderers, tapestry weavers, those working in clay and all those who work with paintbrush and colour'[15] united under the patronage of St Luke. After the conclusion of the truce with Spain, the Rotterdam Guild (1609) adopted the Amsterdam guild's regulations, as did Delft (1611) and Leiden (1615 and 1648); Utrecht had its own version of the guild, while Haarlem revived earlier traditions and was later chosen by the painters' guilds in Alkmaar (1631) and Hoorn (1651) as their model.[16]

In the seventeenth century some guilds were being opened to a wider circle of craftsmen while others limited their membership; finally painters co-operatives were founded. In Delft in 1611, 'all those earning their living here with the art of painting, be it with fine brushes or otherwise, in oil or water-colours; glass makers;

10   Michiel Sweerts, *Drawing a Nude in the Studio*, c. 1656–8, Haarlem, Frans Halsmuseum. (Photo: T. Haartsen)

glass sellers; dish bakers; tapestry makers; embroiderers; engravers; sculptors working in wood, stone or other substance; scabbard makers; art printers; booksellers; sellers of prints and paintings, of whatever kind they many be' were to become members of the guild.[17] Tapestry-makers were excluded from the guild in 1620, but the book-printers were forced to join in 1630 and those who sold faience in 1661. The situation in Leiden, where the painters had no corporate organization, was somewhat different. The glass-makers had founded a Guild of St Luke there in 1615 but they had excluded painters; the painters received the city council's permission to found their own painting guild only in 1648. The guild statutes did not, however, differentiate between artists and house-painters since working with brushes (whatever their size) was considered to be the basic requirement of acceptance into the guild.[18] The artists from the Middelburg Guild of St Luke had failed in their attempt to set up their own guild and separate themselves from the house-painters. The city council refused to give them the permission they needed because they failed to find any plausible reason for founding a second painters' guild.

In the middle of the seventeenth century a process of dislocation set in and many cities began to dissolve their Guilds of St Luke since painters thought that the guild no longer represented their interests. Instead, they founded brotherhoods which were restricted to master-painters. Brotherhoods were founded in Dordrecht in 1642, in Hoorn in 1651 and in The Hague in 1656 (which was called the *Pictura*). In Amsterdam in 1653, a painters' brotherhood – distinct from the Guild of St Luke – had already been set up which guild members could join. In other cities, like Delft, where the artists controlled the organization of the guilds anyway there was no point in leaving the Guild of St Luke.

What were the Guilds of St Luke responsible for? It has already been shown that the guild was involved in the education and training of apprentices. The Guilds of St Luke, like the craft guilds, saw their main role in securing a good living for their members.[19] To achieve this, the differences between rich and poor had to be evened out. Accordingly, the guild's policy was evenly divided between securing and balancing painters' incomes. All of the guild's regulations are unequivocal in this regard. A protection policy could be implemented in many different ways, for example, by binding all those involved in creating art to the guild, which would reduce competition, and by having a monopoly on the local art market. As far as Delft was concerned, the heads of the guild seem to have been in a position to be able to enforce compulsory guild membership for a long time.[20] The artists and craftsmen who lived and worked in Delft (who trained apprentices and sold their output there), were almost totally confined to the guild; only a few printers managed to escape being registered. Towards the end of the seventeenth century, when the guild's regulations were not as strictly observed, some masters managed to establish themselves alongside the guild. However, in general, a sort of social control still functioned among the Delft artisan community.

This was not the case in Amsterdam, where, long before the middle of the seventeenth century, it had been impossible to force people to become members of the guild. Rembrandt, Ferdinand Bol and others worked outside the guild because they did not feel that there was any particular advantage to membership. Unfortunately, this meant that when Rembrandt went bankrupt he had no right to call on the guild's welfare services which, for example, supported Frans Hals in his later years. In Amsterdam an artist did not have to be a citizen in order to work as a painter. Ferdinand Bol, Govert Flinck and Jan van Bronckhorst worked as painters in Amsterdam and, although they were not from there originally, they received important commissions even before they received citizenship together with Jacob van Loo from Sluis, Nicolaes van Helt Stocade from Nijmegen and Jan Asselijn from Dieppe in 1652.[21] The Guilds of St Luke generally tried to increase membership numbers and to have as many masters as possible under their jurisdiction. In Amsterdam, for example, every member contributed four and a half or seven and a half guilders (in Delft six or twelve guilders), to the guild's coffers – depending on whether or not he had been born in the city.[22] Members also had to pay fines for not observing the guild's regulations, fees to use the guild's own studios, and to put by a sum for their own funerals or in case they left the guild.

The guilds were increasing in size because of a growing demand in the art market. If this had not been the case, the guilds would have had to restrict or freeze the number of masters in order to limit the number of pictures that were produced. The prospective master was not required to produce a masterpiece but had to have completed a six-year apprenticeship. In Delft the only craftsmen who were required to produce masterpieces were the faienciers, who were the less privileged members of the guild. However, if they had spent their six years with a Delft master, the guild waived this requirement. This was meant to slow down the influx of foreign faienciers into Delft, which had become a flourishing porcelain centre.

In the long term, the guilds were unable to act as a cartel in the local art market, despite the fact that all the guilds' statutes contained paragraphs forbidding foreigners and non-guild members from selling their art. In Delft, foreign art dealers could advertize their wares twice for twenty-four hours if they paid a fee of one guilder ten stuivers to the guild.[23] However, according to the guilds, the local art markets were not just flooded by offers of works from peripatetic art dealers at fairs, but rather the numer-

ous auctions. Many of the guilds' statutes were devoted to combat-
ing this problem, as were the privileges awarded to them by the
city council against the pervasive influence of the auctions. Since
the number of foreign works of art that the dealers could see was
limited, they then tried to include these goods secretly in the
estate auctions.[24]

In the first half of the seventeenth century, the head of the
Guild of St Luke had already acquired the right to preview
the goods being auctioned. For example, those in charge of the
orphanage were forbidden to begin the auction until a representative of the Guild of St Luke had seen the auction list.[25] In
Delft, on the other hand, foreign pictures could be included in
estate auctions until 1662. The art dealers who were registered
with the guild were, however, allowed to sell imported paintings;
almost half (forty to fifty per cent) of the attributed paintings that
appeared in Delft probate inventories between 1610 and 1680
were painted by artists who had never lived in Delft nor been
members of the local Guild of St Luke.[26] In Amsterdam, between
1620 and 1650, fifty per cent of the pictures in the inventories had
also been painted by artists who did not come from the city.[27] This
demonstrates that though the Guild of St Luke did manage to
limit trading by foreign art dealers, they could not stop the introduction of paintings that had been painted in other cities. In fact,
imported pictures were readily available and there was a lively
demand for them. However, it was not only the urban buyers who
were undermining the guilds' monopoly, the Delft city council
also ordered paintings from foreign artists and thus showed that
they were not restricted to the local Guild of St Luke either. The
guilds' former monopoly, which controlled prices and kept production at a local level, had collapsed a long time before in the
face of market competition. This change meant that, apart from
organizing exhibitions, the guilds' functions were restricted to the
area of providing social services. The guild allocated two-thirds of
its budget to this work since its statutes obliged the leadership to
support guild members who were in need and the guild's poorer
members if they could not find work.

Having looked at painters' social origins and their professional
organization, the next thing to consider is the status of the painter
in Dutch society. As has already been shown, the criteria govern-

11   Jan de Bray, *The Eldermen of the Haarlem Guild of Saint Luke*, 1675, Amsterdam, Rijksmuseum, © Rijksmuseum Stichting.

ing a person's social status were based on wealth and income; the painter's level of education, the number of painters in a city and the artist's role in the eyes of officialdom can also tell us a great deal about his social position.

Firstly, an assessment is made of whether a painter's level of education differed appreciably from that of other comparable social groups. In the fifteenth century, foreign travellers were amazed at the level of literacy in the Netherlands. In the middle of the sixteenth century, an observant commentator, Lodovico Guicciardini, thought that practically everyone in rural areas could read and write.[28] However, this is probably a bit of an exaggeration since, for example, only every second man and every third woman in the 1630 Amsterdam marriage register was able to sign their name. Even considering the fact that many of the painters were immigrants, the level of literacy among the painters is particularly impressive. In Delft, not only all the artists, but practically all the masters of the guild, with the exception of the furniture painters, could read and write.[29] As far as the apprentices were concerned, the degree of literacy depended upon the type of craft that they were learning. Painters, printers and book-binders had received an education, while the majority of the apprentices and journeymen of the faienciers were illiterate. Thus school-learning, no matter how rudimentary it may have been, was a source of personal start-up capital, eventually equipping people to become masters in a painting or craft guild.

Where did accumulating capital come into this scenario? An artist's financial situation could vary considerably during the course of his life. An incredible number of artists were successful and prosperous in the middle of their careers but became impov-erished later on. Rembrandt is the most notable example of this phenomenon, the prominent Delft painters Leonart Bramer and Evert van Aelst met the same financial fate, as did Frans Hals, Jan Steen and Johannes Vermeer, whose position – which was not much to begin with – had worsened dramatically at the end of their lives.

However, these prominent examples should not be allowed to distort our view of the artists' overall level of wealth. Taking the Delft painters as being representative, the details available about the houses they owned, the rent and property tax they paid, the foundations that existed and the painters' estates, can all be used to indicate the economic situation, of both individual artists and the profession as a whole. The guild masters bought and sold houses valued at between 500 guilders, (Cornelis de Man, 1642) and 6,000 guilders (Abraham de Cooge, art dealer, 1644) this allows an average house price of 1,785 guilders to be deter-mined.[30] The master printers of the Guild of St Luke owned the most expensive houses and they were followed by the master-painters. The painters paid the highest recorded level of real-estate tax without reaching the level of taxable land owned by the self-employed – it must be noted, however, that the printers' tax payments have not been recorded. The artists paid an average of 142 guilders per annum in rent, while the house painters rented much cheaper houses (96 guilders per annum).[31]

A second indicator of Delft painters' wealth is shown by the donations that they gave to the city's charitable institution (*Camer van Charitate*), as well as the estates that people left. In the seventeenth century, when someone died in Delft the *Camer* sent a box to the deceased's house and members of the family placed the dead person's best item of clothing in it. When the item of clothing arrived at the *Camer*, the family members could buy it back for a certain amount of money. This means that the size of the donations can be used as an indicator of the deceased's financial circumstances. The list of donations serves to confirm the hierarchy of wealth that was also reflected in the house prices; with the printers at the top, followed by the painters, who gave an average of 120 guilders (even though eight did not contribute at all); they were then followed by the faienciers and the glass-makers.

In terms of studying the social and economic aspects, the probate inventories are even more interesting, although they cannot be used as a comprehensive source because they have not survived intact. Nevertheless those inventories that do exist show that painters had varying amounts of money. The estate of Michiel van Miereveld, who died in 1641 and whose 'picture factory' has already been mentioned, is particularly striking. Miereveld was probably the most successful painter and engraver in Delft during the first part of the seventeenth century.[32] He left two houses, one worth 2,010 guilders and a second that brought in a rent of 180 guilders a year. He also made 1,237 guilders each year from leasing land to farmers. His state and provincial bonds and other capital investments (worth about 14,500 guilders) brought in 900 guilders in interest annually and a further 250 guilders came from private interest-bearing debts. On top of this, he left 5,829 guilders in cash and was owed another 1,200 guilders for pictures. With a total fortune of between 25,000 and 30,000 guilders Miereveld belonged to the richest stratum of the Delft upper class.

In addition to details of Miereveld's estate, the estate auctions of three other painters can also be examined. Willem Jansz. Decker's estate (1642) brought in 857 guilders, Hans Jordaens's (1630) 1,265 guilders, and Cornelis Daemen Rietwijk's (1660) 1,172 guilders – not inconsiderable sums. However, to balance the picture, the case of Evert van Aelst should also be considered. Although he was very successful at first, van Aelst died in poverty in 1657, in a room that he had rented from a tailor; he owned only his painting equipment, a bed, clothes, two portraits and various bits and pieces. His pupil and nephew, Willem van Aelst, who was a successful painter of hunting scenes and floral still lifes in Amsterdam, did not even think it was worth picking up what he had been left, and he refused to accept the inheritance.[33]

These fragments of information can be used to divide the Delft artists and craftsmen into four different social groupings. The first group comprised the consistently successful painters (e.g. Miereveld and Palamedes), sculptors and art dealers (e.g. Johannes Vermeer's father); the rich amateur painters; the owners of book and printing shops and those who owned the faience studios. These formed, so to speak, the top echelons of the guild and lived in houses worth 2,000 guilders or more. If they remained successful to the end of their lives these people possessed a fortune of between 15,000 and 20,000 guilders. The majority of the eldermen of the Guild of St Luke came from this group and were on a level, both economically and socially, with lawyers, doctors, silversmiths and successful merchants.

The second group was made up of the less successful painters, glass-makers, the sculptors who were not self-employed, embroiderers, printers and faienciers who lived in houses worth between 800 and 1,500 guilders and whose personal effects were worth about the same amount. The third group was made up of those who were not yet members of the guild but who could have become masters. They were generally painters' sons and they worked in their fathers' studios or as journeymen for other masters with the result that nothing is known of their economic status. The last group was made up of the vast majority of apprentices and journeymen of the faience industry – these people made up the lower class of the Delft craft community. Based on this reconstruction, the Delft painters belonged to the first two of these groups, however, in order to be a member of a certain group an artist had to be successful and to have established himself as an independent master. If an artist joined the guild as a master and was in tune with the taste of the affluent members of the public, he could rise to be a member of the leading artistic group and even the city's upper class.[34]

Some of the evidence from Amsterdam confirms the impression that has been gleaned from the Delft records as far as the division of wealth is concerned. A tax list for 1631 includes all those who had a fortune of more than 1,000 guilders.[35] All amounts over this sum were taxed at a rate of two per cent, so that it is possible to deduce how much money these people had. For example some of the painters on the list paid:

Gillis de Hondecoeter	5 guilders from 1,250 guilders
Govert Jansz.	5 guilders from 1,250 guilders
David Vinckboons	10 guilders from 1,500 guilders
Jan Jansz. den Uyl	15 guilders from 1,750 guilders
Nicolaes Eliasz.	15 guilders from 1,750 guilders
Arent Arentsz.	20 guilders from 2,000 guilders
Adriaen van Nieulandt	25 guilders from 2,250 guilders

Other well-known Amsterdam painters either did not pay tax, or were forgotten about and not included on the list. The amounts would seem to indicate that painters belonged to the middle class – the class that the painters from Delft belonged to; however, there is no conclusive proof of this.

A painter's income is probably a more reliable indicator of class, but this begs the question of whether or not a seventeenth-century Dutch painter's income can be gauged with any certainty. One thing is clear: that an average artist's income exceeded that of most other craftsmen. This is why, in 1648, the Leiden house-painters complained about the fact that they were expected to pay the same guild membership fees as the artists even though an artist could earn as much in a day as a house-painter could in an entire month and, in addition to this, the house-painter could work only during the three or four driest months of the year. Consequently, the house-painters asked for their membership fees to be reduced.[36]

Michael Montias tried to estimate artists' incomes and their output by extrapolating from their artistic commissions.[37] Contracts concluded between painters and art dealers provide an insight into the income that could be obtained from producing art.[38] In 1625, the artist Jacques de Ville promised to paint Captain Hans Melchiorsz. pictures to the value of 2,400 guilders over a one-and-a-half-year period to settle old debts. Since Melchiorsz. paid for the paints, canvas and frames, the painter earned 1,600 guilders a year. In another contract, Pieter van den Bosch committed himself to paint for Marten Kretzer from 7 a.m. to 7 p.m.

during the summer and from sunrise to twilight in winter for the sum of 1,200 guilders a year. In March 1679, a member of the Grebber family was commissioned to paint six pictures with scenes from the Passion for sixty guilders each, in four to five months – this would have given him an annual income of 800–1,000 guilders. Abraham van de Heck however, who was paid 380 guilders for two portraits within a two-month period, received considerably more; if he had been given such contracts during the whole year this would have amounted to more than 2,000 guilders. Based on these and on other contracts, Montias calculated that by around the middle of the seventeenth century an artist had an annual income of 1,400 guilders, but this was the upper limit. An artist's average net earnings probably ranged from 1,150 to 1,400 guilders. To put this into perspective, this was about three times as much as a master-carpenter earned. Even though one should be careful when making this type of estimate, a painter's earning capacity can be verified by looking at the daily wages. According to his own records, Caesar van Everdingen painted the doors of the organ in the Grote Kerk, Alkmaar in 1643/4 by working for 547 days for a daily wage of three guilders – during the same period a master-carpenter would have received one guilder a day.[39] A hundred years later, when Dutch painting had long passed its zenith, Jan van Gool complained in his *Nieuwe Schouburgh* that by then even a good painter scarcely earned twice that of a carpenter. If this is to be believed, then it would mean that the substantial differences in income between painters and other craftsmen, which have been established for the seventeenth century, diminished in the course of the eighteenth century.

How many painters were there in the Netherlands? The first clue can be seen in the records of the Guild of St Luke (Table 2). When the number of artists is correlated with the estimated population, a painter density is found in the cities that ranges from 0.8 in Leiden to 2.1 per 1,000 inhabitants in The Hague. This difference reflects the demand for art and thus the opportunities for artists which existed in the individual cities. While the city of Leiden, the largest industrial fabric-producing centre in Europe at that time, did not really stimulate artistic production (they formed their own painters guild only in 1648), The Hague, with the court of the House of Orange and the bureaucrats of the

Table 2 Registered artists in Dutch cities around 1650[40]			
City	Artists	Inhabitants	Artists per 1,000 Inhabitants
Alkmaar	24	15,000	1.6
Delft	36	24,000	1.5
Haarlem	68	38,000	1.8
The Hague	37	18,000	2.1
Leiden	55	67,000	0.8
Utrecht	60	30,000	2

States General, was extremely painter-friendly: many artists stopped there on their way to other cities, and stayed for a few years. Unfortunately, there are no specific figures for Amsterdam and the Netherlands as a whole, only estimates.[41] Thus, it is possible to arrive at a total of between 650 and 750 painters in the Netherlands, that is, one painter per 2,000–3,000 inhabitants. These figures are not very helpful in isolation, but they can be informative when compared with another country. Thus they may be compared with Italy at the time of the Renaissance – even though such comparisons are always problematic because of the uncertainty of the sources. Out of a population of 9 million in Renaissance Italy (the population of the Netherlands was 1.85 million), Peter Burke has estimated that there were 313 painters, sculptors and architects, that is, members of the creative élite.[42] Even if this amount is tripled in order to include anonymous artists, it means that there was an artist for every 10,000 inhabitants. Thus it can be seen that the artistic 'density' was much higher in the Netherlands during the seventeenth century and this was based on the high level of urbanization in Dutch society.[43]

The Dutch painter lived in densely-populated cities where there was approximately one painter per 1,000 inhabitants. He met his clients and those who gave him commissions met him on the street, in the tavern and also at the guild's festivities, which were attended by representatives of the city council and the urban upper class. The contemporaneous writers on art and the literary upper class, which have influenced the understanding of the historical reception of Dutch painting up to the twentieth century, show how these social contacts increased the artist's public standing. In particular, the pronouncements of the

art commentators Karel van Mander, Arnold van Houbraken
and Joachim von Sandrart who contrasted the Dutch painter-
craftsman with the ideal of the Renaissance artist are often
quoted. For example, Karel van Mander complained: 'O ungrate-
ful era where under the force of unskilful daubers such shameful
laws and constricting regulations have been brought in that in
almost all the cities the noble art of painting has been forced into
a guild.'[44] While the moralist Jacob Cats with the words *hoe schilder
hoe wilder* (the painter, the savage) ridiculed painters, Constantijn
Huygens, the erudite Secretary of the court of the House of
Orange and Rembrandt's patron, praised the art of painting that
he had been taught in his youth: 'For honor's sake it is enough
that it has the favor of the most powerful lords on earth, either
through being practiced by men of note or by making famous all
those who apply themselves to it with success. It has always produced immeasurable benefit (at least if by that word is understood
the profit from material gain).'[45] Painting was never a career
option for Huygens himself and when his protégé Rembrandt
experienced financial hardship, Huygens did nothing to help
him. The relatives of Rembrandt's wife belonging to the Frisian
Regents, accused him of being a painter; Arnold van Houbraken
and Joachim von Sandrart later stated that Rembrandt 'in the
autumn of his life in the main consorted with mean people and
artists.'[46] Among the contemporary authors, only Jacob Cats
reached a large readership at the time, however the others were to
influence opinions on Rembrandt for posterity.

Joris Craffurd, a contemporary, gave the most accurate description of the class that painters came from, and to which the majority of them belonged 'traders or shop-owners among which many
master craftsmen and craftsmen must be counted'.[47] According to
Craffurd's third level, painters belonged to the middle class which
Groenhuis and Faber later divided into two groups, both socially
and economically. If Faber's division of wealth is applied to
Holland, then the Delft masters would be in the upper middle
class with between 4,000 and 9,000 guilders, whereas, based on
the Amsterdam painters' taxable wealth, they seem to belong to
the lower middle class (1,000–3,000 guilders). This question can
finally be settled only when further regional studies have been
carried out on painters' incomes and wealth. However, a suc-

cessful painter in both Amsterdam and Delft could amass a huge fortune of more than 15,000 guilders. Artistic and financial success changed a painter's life and work; some like Miereveld, Honthorst and Dou organized their studios like large firms with a staff of employees; others like Bol, Hobbema or Terborch married well and then took up an official position or rose to the patriciate in their native cities, either completely gave up painting as a career or limited it.

V

Patronage and the Art Market

In the seventeenth century, commercialization had a wide-ranging effect not only on the economic life of the Netherlands but, for the first time in Europe, also affected art as market forces proved to be more powerful than patronage (which had been the dominant force up until then). The majority of artists worked for an anonymous market which they supplied either directly or through art dealers. However, this did not mean that old-style patronage stopped completely, portrait painters were still dependent on commissions unless they were prepared to paint the mass-produced portraits of the members of the court of the House of Orange. Famous artists like Gerrit Dou, Frans van Mieris and Johannes Vermeer, all of whom were valued because of their personal style, worked almost exclusively and over long periods of time for a single client. Therefore when patronage is mentioned, one should differentiate between public, corporate and private patrons.

Traditionally, the church had been the most important patron, but following the iconoclasm of the Calvinists in the 1560s, the church was no longer a patron of art in the northern Netherlands. Paintings and statues that had survived the iconoclastic attacks were removed from the Reformed churches, the walls of which were whitewashed. The result of this was that the only decorative element that remained in the churches was the organ, and even this was in dispute. This meant that the only commissions the Reformed Church could give were for decorating organs such as, for example, in Alkmaar in 1644 and Amsterdam in 1645.[1]

Compared with the rulers of other European countries, the House of Orange were relatively modest patrons of art, especially with regard to Dutch painters who rarely received commissions from them. The stadholder, Frederick Henry, and his ambitious wife Amalia von Solms tried, in the second quarter of the century, to give the stadholder's court some regal sparkle by commissioning artists and buying seventeenth-century paintings. However, they preferred the Flemish masters Rubens and van Dyck, and the Utrecht School.[2] Gerrit van Honthorst, one of the leading Utrecht Caravaggists, received commissions not only for Honselaardijk Castle but also ousted Miereveld as the portrait painter at the stadholder's court – it seems that Miereveld had, in the meantime, gone out of fashion. Constantijn Huygens had brought Lievens and Rembrandt to the court's attention, they were given commissions and the stadholder also had some of their paintings in his own collection. Rembrandt received six hundred guilders for each of the five paintings that he painted for the stadholder after 1635 – far in excess of what his Leiden clients were prepared to pay for one of his paintings.[3]

The patronage from the court of the House of Orange reached its zenith after the death of Frederick Henry in 1647, with the embellishment of the Oranjezaal in Huis ten Bosch Castle near The Hague. Amalia von Solms dedicated the Oranjezaal to her husband's memory and commissioned the Fleming Jacob Jordaens to direct the restoration.[4] The Flemings – Theodor van Thulden, Thomas Willeboirts Bosschaert, Gonzales Coques – and the Dutch painters Caesar van Everdingen, Salomon de Bray, Jan Lievens, Christiaen van Couwenbergh, Pieter Soutman, Pieter de Grebber and Gerrit van Honthorst were employed to carry out the work under Jordaens's direction.

Owing to the early death of the next governor, Prince William II, who drowned in 1650 aged 24, and to the fact that the post remained unfilled for some time, the Orange family were unable to create a regal Baroque style in the Netherlands. More important, from the point of view of cultural history rather than the history of art, was the patronage of another member of the House of Orange, John Maurice of Nassau-Siegen. After John Maurice had been named stadholder of Brazil by the West Indian Company he took the painters Frans Post and Albert Eeckhout with him on his Brazilian travels as members of his entourage of learned men to record what they saw in the country, both scientifically and artistically. The painters depicted almost everything they saw; Post painted mainly landscapes and Eeckhout people and

12   Frans Post, *Brazilian Landscape with Manor House and Sugar Mill,*
c. 1655, Schwerin, Staatliches Museum.

their work, thus making an important contribution to contemporary Europe's knowledge of Brazil.[5]

Dutch painters received much more support from the various
city and provincial governments than they did from the House of
Orange. This generally came in the form of commissions for
decorating buildings, especially town halls, and sometimes for
gifts for foreign potentates and diplomats. They decorated the
town halls with pictures with an historical-allegorical content, for
example, portraying a just city government interested in the well-
being of the city's inhabitants or reminding people of the Netherlands' early history, for example, the Batavian era and the leader
Claudius Civilis.

The rebuilding of the Amsterdam Town Hall promised to
create a number of commissions, beginning in 1648 with the
plans of the architect Jacob van Campen who tried to combine
Flemish Baroque and Italian Classicism in the building,[6] which, in
turn, needed monumental paintings. As the Amsterdam Guild of
St Luke demanded commissions for local painters, Ferdinand

13   Gerrit Adriaensz. Berckheyde, *The New Town Hall of Amsterdam,*
c. 1675, Schwerin, Staatliches Museum.

Bol, Jan Lievens and Govert Flinck were employed in addition to
the Flemings and members of the Utrecht School. After Flinck's
sudden death, Lievens and Rembrandt were also employed.[7] Bol,
Lievens and Flinck received 1,500 guilders for each picture in the
mayor's rooms. In 1659 Flinck contracted to paint twelve paintings for the gallery at a rate of two paintings a year for 1,000
guilders each, but this never came to fruition.[8] Their client, the
Mayor of Amsterdam, was not happy with the artists' work. They
had no experience in dealing with monumental architecture and
their painting was not to his taste. The result of all this was that the
refurbishment of the town hall was never finished. They even gave
Rembrandt back his painting *The Conspiracy of Claudius Civilis,* to
be reworked and never took it back from him.[9]

  Naturally it was not every day that a town hall was built or
decorated in Holland, and, in general, commissions from the city
magistrates in the other cities were neither numerous nor gen-
erous. In the period 1660–68, Leonart Bramer was the only
person in Delft to get numerous commissions, amounting to

2,330 guilders, a sum that supported him for a long time. Between 1619 and 1675, the city of Delft gave commissions worth a total of only 7,562 guilders, an average expenditure of 135 guilders per annum. Since some of this money went to maritime painters such as Hendrick Vroom and Simon de Vlieger who had either never lived or worked in Delft, or no longer did so;[10] as far as the local professional artists were concerned, municipal commissions generally represented only a bit of extra income, nothing more.

Where did corporate or private commissions come into the scheme of things? This question naturally leads to consideration of the numerous group portraits of the urban militia (*schutters*) or the so-called Regent portraits (*regentenportretten*) which, in terms of the number of paintings, are unique in European art history. The urban militia guilds had, as early as the sixteenth century, already commissioned painters to do group portraits. The fee was based on the number of people in the portrait and each person had to pay for his own likeness. From the commission that the officers of the Amsterdam Crossbow Militia Guild gave to Frans Hals in 1633 for *The Meagre Company*, it can be deduced that they had to pay 60 guilders per figure, that is, a total of 960 guilders for sixteen men. Later the militia raised the price to 66 guilders, but were still unable to get Pieter Codde to finish the portrait begun by Frans Hals, who was then living in Amsterdam.[11] The eldermen of the craftsmen's guilds, like the Amsterdam Coopers' Guild or the Haarlem Guild of St Luke, either arranged commissions for group paintings or painted them themselves. The directors of the charitable institutions also had themselves depicted in Regent portraits (these should not be confused with the paintings of the Regents themselves – the leading political class).

Influential people – whether urban or rural – are rarely found in group paintings: they preferred to have individual portraits painted. This led to an increase in the number of famous portrait painters, and even painters who were less well known could receive lucrative commissions if they were any good at all at portrait painting. By this time, master craftsmen, traders and merchants who had recently married had themselves painted with their wives once they had more than just modest means at their disposal. When they did not have enough money for this, they turned to a less expensive portrait painter who would paint them in a day for six guilders. The other criterion that influenced the price of a portrait was the format (head only, half-length or full figure). In Delft, however, it was possible to have quite a good portrait done for thirty guilders. Wealthy citizens either went to Miereveld or gave commissions to well-known painters in The Hague or Amsterdam, who were much more costly. Rembrandt, for example, demanded a fee of fifty guilders for a head only portrait and up to five hundred guilders for a life-size portrait; half-length portraits and people in group portraits cost one hundred guilders each.[12] Thus the portrait painter could make a good or even a very good living. However, the number of clients was limited, since people generally had themselves painted only when they had a certain amount of money and then just once in a lifetime. The general public was more likely to buy a portrait of a member of the House of Orange – which were also available as prints – than to have their own portraits painted.

The majority of painters did not have any regular commissions from public institutions or private individuals. They produced paintings for an anonymous market and could sell their works in a number of different ways. Painters either sold their work directly to clients who visited their studios, or through the exhibitions and sales organized by the Guild of St Luke; they could also put their paintings into a lottery or have them auctioned. Debts to tavern-keepers and merchants were paid off with paintings and artists used various arrangements made by the art market, from hawkers to established art dealers, to market their artistic output. Contemporary sources provide relatively little information about the paintings that were sold to clients directly in the artist's studio. The painters did not keep sales records, nor did they give their clients receipts. However, the stock of pictures, together with frames, canvases and unfinished works that were found among painters' effects after their deaths leads to the conclusion that the painters did indeed sell pictures directly from their studios.[13]

Exhibitions and sales of works of art were organized by the Guild of St Luke as well as the newly formed painters' brotherhoods, but there is no record of them having taken place in every city. The most extensive records available are for the city of Utrecht where the exhibition was eventually regulated by the magistrate.[14] The guild had already set up a permanent exhibition in an Utrecht convent in 1639/40. The exhibition rooms were divided into different sections where the painters hung their own works. Since the painters were rather reluctant to take part in this enterprize, in 1644 the magistrate gave each painter three months to deliver a painting (which he had painted himself) to the exhibition. This picture then had to remain there until it was sold. When the picture was sold, the painters' guild received five per cent of the price and the picture had to be replaced with another one of a similar value within six months. However, this obligatory payment of five per cent of the sale price to the guild did not really seem to encourage the painters to participate in the exhibition, which remained patchy. Also in 1644, an attempt was made to solve this problem by introducing an auction of the exhibition items every three years, but this did not help the situation very much either. The permanent exhibitions by painters in The Hague seemed to arouse greater interest since they had an affluent set of clients at the Orange Court, among the delegates of the States General and the foreign envoys.

In 1656, when the painters broke away from the Guild of St Luke and founded their own brotherhood, called *Pictura*, they also decided to decorate their assembly rooms with their pictures.[15] Each painter was to contribute a picture and ten per cent from the sale was to go into the brotherhood's coffers. This permanent exhibition seemed to have been accepted by the public: a good one hundred years later, in 1763, the exhibition was extended and there were even regular opening times. However, The Hague was familiar with a tradition of private exhibitions even before the *Pictura* – it is known that in the 1620s the painter Willem Jansz. Decker and the art dealer Pauwel Weyts had already rented the gallery 'between the Great Hall and the Chamber of the States General' otherwise known as the White Gallery of the Orange Court, to exhibit their paintings.[16]

In the seventeenth century, the prizes that could be won in the lotteries were exhibited and this also became a way of exchanging pictures. In no other European country did the lottery system, or rather the lottery scandal, have such strange consequences as in the Netherlands. The lotteries were held either at a municipal or a local level and were organized to fund charitable undertakings such as building orphanages and old people's homes. Buying a lottery ticket allowed people to combine pleasure with altruism since their desire to win was tempered with the knowledge that they were supporting charitable causes. The large prizes that were offered, whether porcelain, paintings or cash, unleashed a real lottery mania, which can be compared to the speculation that took place in tulip bulbs. People bought a lot of tickets in order to increase their chances of winning and paid not only in cash but also in valuables. In this way the lottery system gradually became independent and as far as the people running the lottery were concerned, it turned into a profitable business. Painters and art dealers also used this lucrative opportunity to display their work and stocks of pictures profitably before the general public.

Bredius' detailed description of a lottery in 1626 shows how they were run and the prizes that could be won.[17] In this lottery, which was organized by the master glass-maker Claes Claesz. van Leeuwen, the prizes were worth 1,275 guilders. The tickets cost 25 guilders each and there were only thirty winners. However, if someone did not win anything three times running he was given a painting worth 18 guilders as a consolation prize. The main prize was a painting called *St John the Baptist Preaching* by Abraham Bloemaert (worth 360 guilders); the next three prize-winners received a religious painting by Bartholomeus van Bassen whose staffage had been painted by Esaias van de Velde, each of which was worth between 108 and 162 guilders; other prizes were van Bassen–van de Velde works worth between 46 and 50 guilders and a painting of a kitchen scene by Dirck Govertsz. worth 48 guilders. In all, twelve of the paintings were worth more than the 25 guilders people had paid for a ticket.

The eldermen of the Guild of St Luke were brought in to value the most expensive prizes and the lottery organizer valued the other paintings himself. Since the estimated value of the prizes was meant to equal the total value of the tickets, van Leeuwen made a profit by buying the prizes below their estimated worth. Although some detailed information about other lotteries is available, it is not known exactly how they were organized and run; for example, it is known that the landscape painter Jan Willemsz. Decker organized a lottery in The Hague in 1614 which in all likelihood consisted of his own works, but there is no more information than that.[18] In another draw in Haarlem, in which forty-two paintings by Haarlem painters were offered as prizes, an attempt was made to make the lottery even more attractive by inviting those who bought three or more tickets to a splendid meal. As a rule, paintings were not the only lottery prizes. In the draws that the lottery organizer, Rogier Laurens, arranged all over the Netherlands in the 1620s, the paintings and the alabaster works, which had been brought in by an art dealer, made up only a small percentage of the prizes which generally consisted of jewellery, table silver and mirrors.[19] The painters had different ways of including their paintings in lotteries. They either sold them to an organizer or they organized draws themselves with their own works, or those of their colleagues, as prizes. They were also able to take part in the lotteries organized by the Guilds of St Luke in Haarlem or The Hague.

These lotteries supplemented the picture auctions described, which the Guilds of St Luke arranged and wanted to control.[20] The guilds' efforts can be explained by the fact that, as far as art lovers were concerned, the auctions were one of the most important sources for purchasing pictures. Pictures in every price range could be bought in the weekly estate auctions. As well as this, there were moving auctions, in which a painter sold his stock of pictures if he had to move to another city.

Painters used all of these methods to sell their pictures, they placed their work in other people's estate auctions and sometimes, as Harmen van Bolgersteyn did in Delft in 1628 with works worth between 614 and 621 guilders, even allowed their own work to be auctioned during their lifetime.[21] However, it was usually the artists' widows who profited from the estate auctions. When a painter died there were generally some unfinished pictures in his studio that had to be finished before they could bring any money in at the auction – painting colleagues would be paid to do this. The fact that a painting had been finished by someone else had little, if any, affect on the price, since authenticity was not considered to be as important then as it is now. If a painter wanted to hold an auction because he was giving up his studio or moving to another city, he needed the guild's permission.[22] This rarely posed a problem, provided that the artist was willing not to practise his craft in the city for a long period of time. This regulation was intended to stop any painter taking improper advantage over others, by auctioning off his stock of pictures.

How this was actually put into practice can be seen by looking at the case of The Hague painter Dirck Dalens, who also worked as a schoolmaster. The Guild of St Luke allowed him to have eighty small pictures auctioned on condition that he left The Hague for at least two years and gave thirty-two-and-a-half guilders to the guild. When Dalens sold one hundred pictures instead of eighty he got into trouble with the guild; before the city council he accused the guild of having forced him to sign an impossible contract. But the council made Dalens honour the terms of the contract and he moved to Leiden. However, the Guild of St Luke allowed him to return to The Hague after hearing a petition from his brother-in-law Willem Lucas.

In the end, the guild rules were not implemented very strictly. It would have been impossible for them to have been implemented in every case because there were always opportunities to get around the regulations, for example, fake compulsory auctions took place where a front man who wanted to auction pictures that he owned would pose as a bankrupt; the Guild of St Luke also acted as an auctioneer for people's estates.[23] The guilds were eager to auction collections of painting themselves. They used to send representatives to the houses of the deceased, to talk the widows and heirs into permitting them to auction the paintings. The painters, as well as the general public, could send pictures that they no longer wanted to these auctions. In the eighteenth century, the guild even printed auction catalogues which they sent to collectors, dealers and artists in the Netherlands.

Who bought paintings at these auctions? Only general answers can be given to this question, since auction records were rarely kept. Still, from the Delft records it is known that prosperous citizens bought pictures by Hans Jordaens, Bloemaert and Pieter Stael at the estate auction of a rich widow.[24] Craftsmen who bought paintings at smaller auctions numbered among the buyers. Of course art dealers also bought at auction, especially those who dealt in second-hand clothing, furniture and pictures. These second-hand dealers, *uytdraegsters* were mostly women; they

helped with the administration of the estates and arranged the
sale of reasonably priced pictures between individual sellers and
buyers. Painting collections that were auctioned by art dealers and
collectors should also be mentioned here. This could either mean
auctioning famous estates like that of the art dealer Crijn
Volmarijn and the collector Lucas van Uffelen, or a compulsory
auction, which occured in the case of the dealer Gerrit van
Uylenburgh.

Much can be learnt about art dealing in the Netherlands, and
the market prices, from the inventories for these sales. The auctions of these famous estates caused a sensation because, in a
unique way, they succeeded in bringing together several strands
of the contemporary art world. The auction of Lucas van Uffelen's
collection in 1639 is particularly famous.[25] Rembrandt attended
this auction with Alfonso Lopez, a converted Portuguese Jew who
dealt in ships, weapons, art and gem stones for the French Court.
One of the paintings being auctioned was Raphael's portrait of
Baldassare Castiglione (now in the Louvre). Lopez bought the
painting for 3,500 guilders and Rembrandt sketched it during the
auction. This example alone shows what the prices were like at
these auctions, and it is interesting to note that nothing painted
by a living Dutch painter would have reached such a price.

Before a closer look is taken at the prices of the works of art, it
should be mentioned that painters' transactions were often con-
ducted without cash. Painters considered their work to be either
a valuable asset or a means of exchange, and they used their
paintings to work off loans or to pay for specific goods and services. Tavern debts were often settled with pictures, with the result
that many tavern-keepers – such as Johannes Vermeer's father –
dealt in art as a sideline. At any rate, painters used their paintings
to pay off loans or pay back interest. In 1660, Jan Steen agreed to
pay back the six per cent annual interest on a loan of 450 guilders,
with three portraits.[26] When painters bought houses or had
renovations carried out, they often paid with pictures. Jacques de
Ville paid off 250 guilders annually from a debt of over 1,500
guilders which he had incurred while renovating a house on
Prinsengracht, Amsterdam. Simon de Vlieger entered into a long-
term contract with the Rotterdam art dealer Crijn Volmarijn,
from whom he had bought a house for 900 guilders.[27] He was able

to pay the sum off monthly by delivering a large picture for 31 guilders or a smaller one for 13 guilders or even a marine picture for 13 guilders. This meant that the art dealer had a continuous source of supply, and the painter had his house.

All sorts of other arrangements existed between artists, dealers and craftsmen, and the reason that so much is known about most of them is that those involved often disputed the terms of agreement. In Delft, the embroiderer Ijselsteyn successfully sued the painter Pieter Stael because he had delivered only a *Sodom and Gomorrah*, and not the promised summer and winter landscapes in exchange for a braided pair of red trousers.[28] Pictures were goods which had a commodity value just like a pair of trousers or any other service. A craftsman did not necessarily accept payment in pictures because he really needed them to decorate his house, but probably because he saw them as trade goods, which could be turned into cash at any stage.

Art dealers were, of course, the most important buyers of art; in the Netherlands of the seventeenth century, they can be divided into different categories. The second-hand dealers, the *uytdraegsters*, have already been encountered in the context of the estate auctions. These dealers, who were often illiterate women, came mainly from the lower social classes. Through their involvement with estate auctions they had direct access to the works of art in them, which they either sold or passed on illicitly. The prices that the *uytdraegsters* paid for their pictures at the estate sales – between one and two guilders – seem to suggest that they dealt only in the cheapest works of art.

One rung higher than the second-hand dealers were the craftsmen and business people who dealt in art as a sideline. The more prominent among them were the tavern-keepers, who displayed their clients' works in their taverns, whether they had been paid for or received in lieu of any debts; and then sold them to other customers. Wine dealers and craftsmen also dealt actively in works of art. Some of them, such as the Antwerp cooper Adrian Delen, even set up a system for producing paintings. In 1615, the marine painter Jan Porcellis, from Leiden, concluded a contract with Delen that required him to paint ships or ship scenes on forty wooden tablets at a rate of two pictures a week. The painter received at least fifteen guilders a week and also shared in the profits, provided that they exceeded the cost of the materials which Delen had paid for.[29] There were also craftsmen working as art dealers as part of their occupation: engravers, printers, frame-makers and less successful artists resorted increasingly to dealing in art if they could not earn a good enough living from painting.

Even prominent art dealers such as Gerrit van Uylenburgh, Cornelis Doeck, Abraham de Cooge, Crijn Volmarijn, Albert Meyeringh and Jan Coelenbier began as less than successful painters. In order to deal in art professionally, one needed to join the Guild of St Luke. According to statements in the guild documents, this first occured on a large scale in the 1630s and 40s, when the high demand for art made it possible for people to earn an independent living by dealing. The Vermeer family is a good example of the progression from second-hand dealer to art dealer. Johannes Vermeer's grandmother, Neeltge Goris, had been an *uytdraegster*, his father Reynier Jansz. Vermeer dealt in pictures as a tavern-keeper and during his own lifetime when he was older, Vermeer himself traded modestly in art, while his brother-in-law, Anthoni Gerritzen van der Wiel, who made ebony frames, was registered in the Delft Guild of St Luke as an art dealer.[30]

From where did art dealers get their wares? To replenish their own stock of pictures, they bought at estate auctions, in particular at other art dealers' estate auctions. Some of the people who bought pictures from the estate of the widow of the art dealer Crijn Volmarijn are listed below:

Abraham Saftleven	180 pictures for 357 guilders 7 stuivers
A. Caijmax	105 pictures for 208 guilders 18 stuivers
Ditto	12 pictures for 42 guilders
Jan Molijn	21 pictures for 92 guilders
Michel Marinus	17 pictures for 48 guilders 18 stuivers

In addition to this, the widow's brother-in-law, Leendert Volmarijn, had already acquired framed and unframed pictures worth 1,034 guilders and 10 stuivers.[31] This shows how many pictures art dealers could have in stock, and how inexpensive these pictures could be. Dealers also increased their stock by employing copyists or painters, as did Martin Kretzer with Pieter van den Bosch in 1645 who, for a steady wage, painted whatever

that the dealer commissioned from dawn to sunset.[32] The independent painters were contemptuous of this way of producing
art and called it *schilderen op de galey* (galley-slave painting). The
painters who had a regular arrangement with art dealers fared
better, even so, payment often varied. In 1641 Isaac van Ostade
received only twenty-seven guilders for thirteen pictures which
Leendert Volmarijn had commissioned him to paint. The painter's brother Adriaen thought that this wage of two guilders per
picture was so low that he sued Volmarijn on his brother's behalf.
The court found for the plaintiff and set a wage of six guilders for
nine of the thirteen pictures.[33]

This was how prominent art dealers like Hendrick van
Uylenburgh built up a kind of artistic business with services that
ranged from stockpiling works of art to arranging the painting of
good-quality portraits.[34] However, this does not mean that the
majority of art dealers had their pictures painted by their own in-
house painters; bigger dealers naturally bought directly from the
painters themselves. They dealt not only in contemporary Dutch
art, they also stocked works of the Italian and Flemish Schools, as
well as offering their clients – at least as copies – the masters of the
Renaissance.[35] In contrast, the smaller art dealers, who satisfied
the mass-market demand, sold only the works that were produced
by the painters who worked for them.

There is one other group of art dealers who dealt in locally-
produced paintings in the middle range, in terms of both quality
and price, and also in art that was not local, for example, by
importing Haarlem landscapes, still lifes, and genre scenes into
Amsterdam. What differentiates the dealers is the source of their
acquisitions which, in turn, led to different marketing strategies.
While the best way for the second-hand dealers to make money
was by going to the fairs and street trading, the art dealers like
Leendert Volmarijn travelled from fair to fair because on fair days
they were allowed to sell paintings in cities where they were not
resident. Since the rural population also came to the fairs, the
dealer had more chance of selling his goods. The clients of the
most prominent dealers were the collectors from the upper-class.
These clients, who were known as *lief-hebbers* (connoisseurs),
visited artistic establishments and allowed the dealers to advise
them. If dealers did not have the piece a client wanted in stock,

then they would either commission a painter who was working for them to produce one or act as an intermediary between painter and client. Many dealers also sent printed catalogues to potential clients.

A successful art dealer had clients not only in Holland but also in Flanders and Brabant. The biographies of two prominent dealers demonstrate how the system worked and how thin the line between success and failure could be. Johannes de Renialme was an important art dealer to the Amsterdam upper class. He had not started out as a painter but had traded in anything and everything before moving on to dealing in art and gems. His stock of paintings is known about because, owing to his lack of capital, he pawned some of them in 1640.[36] He had more that thirty landscapes by Hercules Seghers (the most expensive was worth thirty guilders), a priest by Rembrandt (costing one hundred guilders, this was the most expensive of all the pictures), floral still lifes by Ambrosius Bosschaert, genre paintings by Molenaer, landscapes by van Goyen, Poelenburgh, and Govert Jansz., and marine paintings by Porcellis, all of them modestly priced.

When he died in 1657, Renialme was in a very different situation. According to statements on the estate inventory, Renialme's business had taken a definite turn for the better in terms of his stock, in both quality and price. There are numerous masterpieces among the four hundred pictures, many of which are still to be found in famous collections today, such as Rembrandt's *Christ and the Woman Taken in Adultery* (now in the National Gallery, London) which was, at 1,500 guilders, the most expensive painting. In addition to Rembrandt, practically everyone who was anyone was represented: Terborch, Steen, Potter, Hals, Dou, Rubens, van Dyck, Holbein, Claude Lorrain, Titian, Bassano, and Palma among others. In total, the artistic estate was worth 36,512 guilders. The average price of a picture was 64.1 guilders (105.8 guilders for a signed work, 28.5 for an unsigned one). The estate also contained pearls and precious stones worth 22,000 guilders.[37]

The works of art that were auctioned after the dealer Gerrit van Uylenburgh had to declare bankruptcy were worth even more. The estimated value of the signed paintings averaged out at 135.6 guilders per picture. As well as pictures belonging to the Dutch School and some Italian ones, van Uylenburgh had many paintings among his stock that were marked with notations such as 'in the style of Tintoretto' or 'in the style of Rubens' identifying them as copies. There was a particular reason for this, the roots of which lay behind the bankruptcy. Van Uylenburgh's art business had existed since the 1630s.[38] Hendrick van Uylenburgh, Gerrit's father, financed the business by borrowing money from Dutch painters – among them Rembrandt and Simon de Vlieger – as well as his Mennonite co-religionists. Rembrandt was the artistic soul of the enterprise, he and van Uylenburgh co-ordinated the work of the apprentices and assistants. Van Uylenburgh not only sold the paintings, but was also responsible for having paintings and copies made on a grand scale. Portrait commissions were arranged, etchings were produced and edited, expert reports written, and art lessons for amateurs arranged. After his father's death, Gerrit took over the business (Rembrandt had already left in 1635). Gerrit expanded the trade, turned it into an international business and received commissions from the States General. In 1671, he offered the Great Elector of Brandenburg thirteen paintings by famous Italian painters for 30,000 guilders. In Berlin, they were examined by the flower painter Hendrick van Fromantiou who said they were copies. The paintings were sent back to Amsterdam where the matter triggered a dispute between the experts. Thirty-one of the fifty-one artists who were consulted decided in van Uylenburgh's favour, that is, that the paintings were genuine, but twenty decided against him.

Van Uylenburgh's reputation as a serious dealer was ruined and he had to declare bankruptcy. This dispute reveals something of the practices in the contemporary art market – copies were sold as originals, and names of painters that were no longer fashionable were deleted and sometimes also replaced by those of painters who were in demand. This was how the growing demand of the *nouveau riche* – the name buyers, who demanded old masters and were not interested in contemporary Dutch art – was satisfied. As far as these people were concerned, a painter became interesting only once he was either dead or had ceased to paint. This preference for the so-called old masters, which was encouraged by the art dealers, is clearly reflected in the collections. According to information from the Amsterdam estate inventories, the price of paintings by a deceased master increased substantially towards the

end of the seventeenth century.[39] Since the supply of these
paintings was limited and non-renewable, the art dealer's position
in the art market became more important. But this meant that
the active contemporary painters were at a considerable disadvantage, since the shrinking market meant that they became
more and more dependent on private commissions and the art
dealers.

Finally, the prices that were paid for works of art should be
mentioned. One of the simplest ways of doing this is to compare
the price for art on the open market with the general development of prices in the Netherlands, and also, to compare the prices
of the different artistic genres. Many specific prices for pictures
have already been mentioned and it has thus been made apparent
that some pictures changed hands for one or two guilders but also
that painters like Gerrit Dou received between six hundred and
one thousand guilders for a painting. Even though it is difficult to
contain both sorts of prices within the same scale, they do make
one aware of the great discrepancy between mass-produced art
and individual fine paintings. Naturally these values do not provide very much information about the general development of
prices in the art market, in order to discover this a series of prices
can be used to calculate average prices over a longer period of
time. Accordingly, the most important sources are the prices paid
at auctions and the valuations of the estate inventories. Unfortunately, neither of these sources can be regarded as totally reliable.
The available auction prices are not only sketchy – they were also
strongly influenced by the type of collection that was being auctioned. The estate inventories mirrored the wealth of their
deceased owners and thus the prices of the pictures increased in
proportion to the worth of the estate as a whole. However, the
valuations of the estate inventories (even though they do not
exactly deal with the cheapest pictures), still provide the best
overview of long-term price fluctuations in the art market.

Price was dependent upon the picture's format, its execution
(original or copy) and whether it could be attributed to a known
painter. However, since not all the necessary data is available,
average prices can be calculated only in order to gauge developments in the art market. Thus the 312 paintings that Montias
collated from the Amsterdam estates in the 1640s cost an average

of 6.8 guilders. This figure, however, hides the vast differences in price from 3.21 guilders for smaller pictures (*kleijne schilderijen*) up to 43.8 guilders for big pictures.[40] The prices paid at The Hague auction in 1647 tend to confirm these findings. Here the 850 originals reached a higher price of, on average, 9.3 guilders, as opposed to the copies which averaged out at 4.13 guilders. This means that in the middle of the seventeenth century pictures worth ten guilders could often be found in Dutch households.[41]

Alan Chong, in his studies of the long-term developments in the art market, has concentrated on the higher price categories. This is due in part to the limited number of inventories cited whose prices are known about and also to the fact that they do not include cheap copies.

Table 3   Average prices in guilders of pictures by subject 1600–1700[42]

Subject-matter	1600–25	1626–50	1651–75	1676–1700
Landscapes	30.31	21.77	24.29	43.99
Religious subjects	33.03	43.26	70.26	52.13
Histories	47.60	38.39	44.09	65.29
Portraits	5.99	10.74	23.03	37.05
Genre	27.79	22.07	30.79	88.23
Still lifes	27.39	30.13	23.84	41.33
Architectural subjects	41.43	59.34	52.71	22.50
Other subjects/Unknown	10.55	17.25	20.99	33.00

Table 3 shows the development of prices for individual subjects on the art market between 1600 and 1700. Firstly, it is noticeable that prices varied according to subject. In the first quarter of the century, paintings with a historical subject were the most expensive, followed by religious subjects, architectural subjects and landscapes – including seascapes. These in turn were followed by genre paintings, still lifes and portraits. Fifty years later, in the last quarter of the seventeenth century, the order had changed. Genre paintings were then the most expensive, followed, as was earlier the case, by histories, religious subjects and landscapes, still lifes and portraits; there seems to have been hardly any demand for architectural subjects at this time. Even though there was an increase in the total level of prices in the final quarter, the way in which the prices developed in the different genres is evident. Religious paintings, genre scenes and portraits became more expensive. The price of histories and architectural paintings remained more or less constant, while for twenty years still lifes and landscapes had became cheaper.

Fig. 14   Relative prices of seven commodities in five-year averages 1530–34 to 1720–24 (from J. de Vries)   (1–40 = prices in guilders)

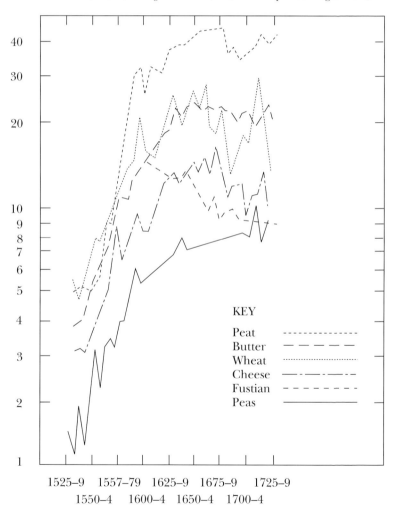

KEY

Peat	----------------
Butter	— — — — —
Wheat	··················
Cheese	—·—·—·—··
Fustian	– – – – – – –
Peas	————————

If one compares the price of pictures with the development of commodity prices in general, they have very few points in common. The prices for grain, butter, cheese and turf rose until about 1650 and then began to fall until the beginning of the eighteenth century. Foodstuffs were cheaper, which meant that people were able to use their money to buy other things as well. This could explain the overall increase in the total value of the art market in the later years of the seventeenth century. However, it is possible that the appreciably higher prices that appear at this time were influenced by the growing number of old masters in the inventories. Faced with a general increase in prices in the first part of the century, the subjects whose prices remained relatively stable became cheaper for the buyers, in relative terms. Some subjects, such as landscapes, had also become much cheaper in real terms, but this was probably caused by innovations in the way in which they were produced.

Innovations in painting technique cut down the time that was needed to produce a painting, consequently landscapes became cheaper.[43] Esaias van de Velde and Jan Porcellis's invention of the so-called tonal style of painting in land- and seascapes was a crucial factor in this development. In contrast to their Mannerist predecessors, they replaced a linear depiction and additive technique with a more painterly technique, representing nature in grey, brown and yellow tones. François Knibbergen, Jan Porcellis and Jan van Goyen are said to have taken only a day to paint their best pictures. Jan van Goyen and Pieter de Molijn were particularly expert in this technique in the 1630s and 40s, and thus managed to increase their output.

Van Goyen painted 1,200 paintings during his artistic life. The supply of landscapes was more extensive, individual pieces were cheaper and ordinary people preferred to buy the new tonal paintings. Landscapes such as those by Gillis van Coninxloo, Gillis de Hondecoeter and Roeland Savery that were painted in a stylized manner, decreased both in number and price.[44] Compared with the pictures of van Goyen, Porcellis, Molijn, Everdingen, Ruisdael and van Goor (who is practically unknown today), they appeared less and less often in the collections. However, there were significant price changes in this group, depend-

15   Jan Porcellis, *Warship and Fishing Vessels near the Coast*, c. 1625, Hamburg, Peter Tamm Collection.

16   Gillis van Coninxloo, *Landscape with Hunters*, c. 1605, Schwerin, Staatliches Museum.

ing on the painting's subject-matter, format and whether or not the painter was fashionable (Table 4).

Paintings by Jacob van Ruisdael and Allart van Everdingen reached quite good prices, while a painting by van Goyen was

Table 4	Price of landscapes by certain painters 1600–1725 (in guilders)[45]					
Painter	1600–25	1626–50	1651–75	1676–1700	1701–25	Highest prices
Gillis van Coninxloo		58.5 (25)	38 (3)	20.3 (8)		350 (1607), 400 (1612), 120 (1620)
Albert Cuyp			26.6 (5)	13.5 (12)		80 (1675), 13 (1688)
Allart van Everdingen			36.1 (23)	8.5 (18)		150 (1657), 100 (1670, 1671)
Jan van Goyen		16.8 (37)	17 (11)	7.7 (9)		32 (1647), 650* (1651), 48 (1657)
Meindert Hobbema			14 (2)			20 (1644, 1693)
Gillis de Hondecoeter	54 (4)	34.3 (9)	35.8 (6)	14.4 (6)		90 (1621, 1657), 150 (1647)
Philips Koninck			74.9 (10)	7 (3)	6.2 (3)	130 (1657), 199 (c. 1670)
Jan Lievens			100.4 (5)	18.4 (5)		200 (1657)
Pieter de Molijn		18.1 (10)	13.9 (15)		6 (4)	50 26,5 ?? (1647)
Cornelis van Poelenburgh		30 (13)	92.4 (7)	106.7 (7)	215 (7)	575* (1627), 120 (1637), 300 (1649), 700 (1673), 360 (1692)
Jan Porcellis		87.2 (12)	84.7 (13)	26.1 (10)	6 (4)	450 (1649), 300 (1657)
Frans Post				59 (5)		180* (1650), 130 (1687)
Paulus Potter			106.5 (4)	28.1 (4)		400* (1652), 80 (1687)
Jacob Pynas						59 (1625), 42 (1693)
Rembrandt						166 (1644)
Roeland Roghman				19.9 (6)		30 (1669, 1681)

continued on next page

Jacob van Ruisdael			42.3 (18)	28.1 (7)		60 (1664), 100 (1673), 80 (1699)
Roeland Savery	68.4 (6)	75.5 (10)	38.6 (6)	34 (2)		255 (1625), 700* (1626), 150 (1627, 1657)
Hercules Seghers		18.5 (36)	70.1 (10)			60 (1654), 300, ?? 100 (1657)
Esaias van de Velde		22.4 (7)		10 (2)		70 (1649)
Hendrick Vroom	46.2 (5) 1,000*	23.2 (4) 287.5 (4)	21 (2)			1,800 (1610), 200 (1616) 750 (1629)
Philips Wouwermans			47.3 (13)	60.1 (20)	195 (4)	90 (1652), 150 (1669), 355 (1687), 255* (1712)

relatively inexpensive. This may have been because the format of van Goyen's paintings was relatively small, but is also due to the fact that they were often copied by other painters and copyists. Works by his tonal colleagues Salomon van Ruysdael and Pieter de Molijn were sold for the same sort of prices; Albert Cuyp's animal landscapes were astonishingly cheap,[46] as they were rarely found outside his home town of Dordrecht, and because animal landscapes were generally the cheapest type of landscape painting. Seascapes and marine paintings were considerably more expensive, costing almost twice as much as all the other landscape paintings, owing to their popularity, larger format and the fact that painting ships and their rigging was very time-consuming.

The only way to reconstruct the influence price exerted on the buying patterns of the Dutch is to analyse the collections. However, it can be stated with certainty that painters' artistic production expanded considerably from the 1630s, in a way that would not earlier have been possible. Innovative techniques and specialization in certain genres increased the supply of works of art on the market. All of a sudden, social groups that would previously have had to make do with copies or prints, could afford originals. When the market was finally satiated – as happened in the last third of the seventeenth century – new marketing strategies had to be introduced. The marketing of the old masters falls into this category, as does the propagation of the new fine style. Even though this fine painting had developed alongside the mass-production approach to art, discerning individuals evolved a taste for finely crafted paintings. One could purchase these pictures from an art dealer or even directly from the artist himself who produced only three or four paintings a year and was therefore dependent on private commissions and the advance payments that went with them. Thus, at the end of a century dedicated to the commercialization of art, patronage had, in fact, become more and more frequent.[47]

17   Rembrandt van Rijn, *Moses with the Tablets*, 1659, Berlin, Gemäldegalerie Staatliche Museen Preußischer Kulturbesitz. (Photo: J. P. Anders)

VI

Collections and Collectors

The Dutch Republic was unique in the number of paintings that were owned by private individuals, and also in the millions of paintings that were produced. Works of art, ranging from simple prints and copies to original paintings, hung in almost all Dutch houses; it is estimated, for example, that pictures of some kind were found in about two-thirds of Delft households.[1] Reconstructing the collections would provide evidence of the painters' output, the artistic taste of the Dutch people and the functions performed by works of art. In the majority of cases, however, it is not known which paintings hung on Dutch walls nor who painted them, nor can any conclusions be drawn from the paintings that are currently in museum collections, since probably less than one per cent of seventeenth-century pictures have survived.[2]

Which sources can be consulted in order to be able to reconstruct Dutch patterns of picture ownership during the seventeenth century? Contemporary descriptions of the famous collections do exist (for example, the cabinet of the Reynst brothers – Gerard and Jan) as do salesroom lists of important collections that were compiled when paintings were auctioned after the deaths of the owners or their widows. Abraham Bredius published lists of most of these collections.[3] However, he was interested in different aspects of the art market than perhaps would be emphasized nowadays. Focussing on works of art owned by painters and also on paintings held in established private collections – which are, of course, important from the art-historical point of view – the Bredius inventories tend to provide information about the relationship between the painter and the collector and about the upper end of the art market, rather than reflecting what kind of art was owned by Dutch society in general.

In order to delve into the depths of the art market and to find out who owned which pictures one has to refer to the general records of the probate inventories, which have been preserved in the national records and have already proved invaluable in determining the social status of painters. About two thousand of these probate inventories exist, from Amsterdam, Delft and Leiden, and they enable the paintings to be viewed from an art-historical perspective. Despite the fact that they were compiled by notaries, these sources are not without their problems,[4] the most fundamental one being that the authenticity of the information about the pictures mentioned in the probate inventories depends a great deal on the value of the estate. In less valuable estates, that is those under 1,000 guilders, the inventories give only general descriptions such as 'a picture (*schilderij*), a panel (*bort*), a portrait (*tronie*)', details that are not particularly helpful for attempting a complete analysis. In contrast, notes on the genre, such as landscape, seascape, kitchen scene, still life or biblical scene, are a great deal more helpful, as they allow for the reconstruction of preferences for certain subjects at different times.

Attributing a painting to a particular painter, however, poses some difficulties. Attributed pictures are generally found only in the more valuable estates, that is those with a value of about 2,000 guilders or more, the pictures of which would generally have been valued by the eldermen of the Guild of St Luke if they were going to be auctioned. But these more valuable estates are insignificant in terms of Dutch society as a whole, since they represent the households of wealthy citizens from the middle and upper classes. Accordingly, in order to find out more about the ownership of art over a broader social spectrum, the different genres of painting found in collections need to be studied.

To start with, however, the large number of pictures in the inventories – which in itself seems astonishing – has to be examined. For example, the average number of paintings in individual Delft inventories rose from ten in the 1610s to twenty in the 1670s, and Amsterdam inventories show a rise from twenty-five to forty paintings during the same period.[5] So it was no wonder that in 1643 a Leiden cloth-dyer possessed sixty-four paintings, and two other dyers in the 1670s possessed ninety-six and one hundred and three paintings each.[6] The probate inventories clearly show the kind of paintings that the Dutch hung in their houses. Five main subjects can be differentiated: (1) histories, including subjects from the Bible, history, mythology and allegories; (2) landscapes, including seascapes and sea battles; (3) still lifes; (4) genre paintings; (5) portraits.

Table 5   Paintings in the Delft inventories 1610–1679[7]

Subject-matter	1610–19		1620–29		1630–39		1640–49		1650–59		1660–69		1670–79	
	No.	%	No.	%	No.	%	No.	%	No.	%	No.	%	No.	%
Histories	218	46.1	547	44.5	550	41.1	754	34.3	470	26.1	441	26.3	170	16.6
Landscapes	121	25.6	290	23.7	369	27.6	573	26.1	610	33.9	606	38.6	419	40.9
Still lifes	20	4.2	137	11.2	133	9.9	256	11.7	247	13.7	242	15.4	171	16.7
Genre	18	3.8	56	4.6	61	4.6	82	3.7	88	4.9	76	4.8	76	7.4
Portraits	80	16.9	166	13.6	185	13.8	479	21.8	329	18.3	192	12.2	154	15.0
Others	16	3.4	29	2.4	40	3.0	49	2.2	58	3.2	39	2.5	35	3.4
Totals	473		1,225		1,338		2,193		1,802		1,566		1,025	

Table 6   Paintings in the attributed Amsterdam estates 1620–1689[8]

Subject-matter	1620–29		1630–39		1640–49		1650–59		1660–69		1670–79		1680–89	
	No.	%	No.	%	No.	%	No.	%	No.	%	No.	%	No.	%
Histories	227	46.9	404	32.4	412	23.8	268	16.1	282	14.2	278	15.5	112	11.6
Landscapes	98	20.2	315	25.3	467	27.1	474	28.5	660	33.2	568	32.2	353	36.5
Still lifes	30	6.2	100	8	157	9.1	144	8.7	202	10.2	159	9	72	7.4
Genre	19	3.9	86	6.9	141	8.2	123	7.4	157	7.9	182	10.3	116	12
Portraits	73	15.7	193	15.4	292	16.9	326	19.7	336	17	268	15.2	98	10.1
Others/ Unknown	36	7.1	150	12	257	14.9	326	19.6	350	17.5	309	17.8	215	21.4
Total	483		1,248		1,726		1,661		1,987		1,764		966	

When the development of genres in the seventeenth-century inventories from Delft and Amsterdam is followed (Tables 5 and 6), two distinct trends can be seen: on the one hand, the continuous reduction in the number of histories and, on the other, the unstoppable increase in the number of landscapes. In the first third of the seventeenth century, nearly half of the collections (forty-five per cent) were still composed of histories, but towards the end of the century this position was usurped by landscapes,

and only one-tenth of the pictures in the inventories were histories. The main reason for the relative loss of significance of history
paintings was the reduction in biblical subjects. Scenes from the
Old and New Testaments – which had accounted for one-third of
all the paintings in private collections at the beginning of the
seventeenth century – now played only a secondary role. Paintings
with a historical, mythological or allegorical content were significant only in the more valuable inventories, that is, in wealthy and,
presumably, educated families. The increase in the popularity of
landscapes cannot be explained in the same way as the decline in
the popularity of histories. Though notaries often described a
picture as a landscape it is not known whether this term was also
being used for a seascape or a coastal scene. Seascapes, reflecting
perhaps the growing number of registered sailors, became more
and more popular in the course of the seventeenth century.

In third place in the popularity stakes are portraits, but towards
the end of the century, they were overtaken by genre paintings. In
the first half of the century the need for personal recognition had
created a market for the portrait painters, and consequently the
number of portraits in households increased. By the late seventeenth century personal portraits seem to have gone slightly out of
fashion, and the number of artists specializing in portraits also
decreased. Towards the end of the century, at least in Amsterdam,
still lifes seem to have lost some of the popularity that they had
first gained in the middle of the century. The subject-matter
within the heterogeneous group of still-life paintings also under-
went a change. Fruit and floral still lifes became more popular,
while the number of kitchen still lifes as well as the breakfast,
banquet, vanitas and fish still lifes decreased – especially in the
second half of the century.[9]

The final type of painting to consider is genre painting which
has profoundly influenced the present-day concept of
seventeenth-century Dutch painting. Genre painting's share of
space within collections increased steadily from 3.9 per cent
(1620–29) to 12 per cent (1680–89). Second to landscapes, genre
paintings were the most frequently mentioned in the inventories
by the end of the seventeenth century. The general term 'genre
painting' covers various subjects, such as the peasant pieces
(*boertjes*) that were very popular during the whole of the seven-

18   Ambrosius Bosschaert the Elder, *Vase with Flowers*, c. 1620, The Hague, Mauritshuis.

teenth century, happy gatherings (*geselschapjes*), brothel scenes (*bordeeltjes*) and, especially in the second half of the century, guard-room pictures (*corte-gaerdjes*).[10]

Interestingly, the change in subject-matter evident in the private Amsterdam and Delft collections is, in part, reflected by art ownership in Leiden, as well as in the trends in the art market, which Alan Chong has reconstructed with the information derived from picture prices.[11] Thus the increase in the value of genre paintings can be explained by the increasing demand for this type of picture, and by the reduction in the price of still lifes because they were no longer fashionable. However, this should not be confused with the reduction in the price of landscapes – a result of the changes in the way that they were produced – which had had the effect of stimulating demand. Thus supply and demand within the art market were reflected in many different ways, in both the price and ownership of paintings.

Which painters were represented in Dutch households? From examining the pictures in the Amsterdam inventories, it can be seen that Jan Molenaer, Rembrandt, Gillis de Hondecoeter, Joos de Momper, Jan Porcellis and Philips Wouwermans are each mentioned thirty-five to forty-one times, and between them they painted about ten per cent of all the attributed paintings in the inventories. However, the number of inventories in which a master-painter appeared is not necessarily an indication of his popularity or output. In the leading group, mentioned in eighteen to twenty-five inventories, not only Jan Molenaer and Joos de Momper are found, but also Pieter Aertsen, Roeland Savery, Jan van Goyen and Jan Pynas.[12] In the inventories, and therefore in the Amsterdam collections, the artists who appeared most often were quite famous in the Netherlands, but the great majority of them did not work as master-painters in Amsterdam.[13] By contrast in Delft (where the buyers still knew the local painters), of the twenty painters mentioned in the inventories most often, only two, van Goyen and de Momper were not masters in the Delft Guild of St Luke. The Delft inventories include well-known painters – a total of 1,962 attributions – however, Rembrandt is mentioned only seven times, Frans Hals once and even Johannes Vermeer, the head of the local Guild of St Luke, only once in the 1660s.[14] The number of Italian masters who appear in the Delft

19   Adriaen Brouwer, *Inn with Drunken Peasants*, c. 1625, The Hague, Mauritshuis.

inventories is similarly small, and the Amsterdam inventories record fifteen 'originals'. Copies of works by contemporary Flemish and Utrecht School painters are also found in the Amsterdam inventories – works that would have been quite expensive as original paintings.

The inventories also provide information on the age of paintings in each collection. Were the collections composed of paintings purchased during the painter's actively creative period, or were the painters no longer alive in the decade in which the inventory was compiled? According to information in the Amsterdam inventories, paintings in the collections became older throughout the seventeenth century: whereas two-thirds of the pictures in the inventories from the 1630s were painted by contemporary artists, in the 1670s the number of painters mentioned who were still painting had fallen to forty per cent and the old masters predominated. There may be many reasons for this phenomenon. On the one hand, in the 1630s more collections were compiled from current works of art than later on and, on the other, artistic output decreased in the latter part of the seventeenth century, since the buyer's taste – as van Gool complained in the beginning of the eighteenth century – had turned deliberately towards the older and more expensive masters.[15]

As a result one must look for criteria that will enable the classification of the owners of paintings in seventeenth-century Dutch society. One criterion that was insignificant with regard to the art lover's social status, but which did play a role in picture purchasing, was religion. Thus one can collate the Amsterdam inventories on the basis of their owners' religion (159 Calvinist, 43 Catholic).[16] Apart from the fact that the Catholic, as well as Calvinist collections, also reflected the long-term trend away from histories towards landscapes, there were some significant differences with regard to subject-matter. Calvinist collections were marked by a greater number of landscapes and still lifes, whereas Catholics preferred histories, in particular subjects from the New Testament. Calvinists, who were forbidden to venerate pictures, very rarely hung scenes from the New Testament on their walls. Hence the devotional pictures that were venerated by Catholics, such as Crucifixion scenes or paintings of the Virgin Mary, were as unlikely to be found in Calvinist collections as pictures of Sts Peter and Paul. In contrast, the Orthodox Calvinists preferred figures from the Old Testament such as Abraham, and Lot and Moses, as well as the political portraits of members of the House of Orange; whereas portraits of the Counts of Brabant or Charles V were hung in Catholic households.

The inventories can be interpreted in terms of their owners' social status only to a limited extent. However, one can correlate the prices of pictures in Delft with the value of the estates and, in the case of Amsterdam, the more valuable paintings can be compared with the less important estates (those without attributed paintings). In addition, the cream of the collectors and their pictures are known about. In the simpler Delft estates, which were worth less than five hundred guilders, copies and cheap pictures worth between one and two guilders predominated.[17] The price of pictures in the estates was linked to a rise in the value of the owner's possessions in general, so, for example, pictures for five to ten guilders were found in the estates worth five hundred to one thousand guilders. The majority of artisans, who could seldom

20   Jan van Goyen, *View of the Haarlem Sea*, 1656, Frankfurt, Städelsches Kunstinstitut. (Photo: U. Edelman)

afford to pay more than ten guilders for a picture, left this sort of estate when they died. However, it was still possible to buy a small van Goyen for ten guilders, even if people from Delft preferred their local painters.

People whose estate passed the one thousand guilder threshold had their walls decorated during their lifetimes with large-format paintings by the masters of the Guild of St Luke, and they may even have purchased one of the better copies of paintings in the Flemish or Utrecht style. In terms of subject-matter, the modest Amsterdam estates can be compared with the Delft estates of two thousand guilders or more. It is interesting to observe that histories were also gradually being replaced by landscapes in the less valuable collections. However, this change took place more slowly than in the valuable collections, so that the less valuable collections seem more traditional. For example, subjects from the Old and New Testaments in unattributed paintings in inventories from 1620 to 1649 made up 30.9 per cent of these collections, whereas these subjects constituted only 19.8 per cent of the more valuable collections. Also, the wealthier collectors tended to be more educated, or at least liked to pretend that they were, and they owned more pictures representing scenes from ancient mythology.

Over and above even these more valuable collections containing attributed pictures were those of famous collectors whose best pieces alone were worth many thousands of guilders. Many of the paintings that such collectors purchased were Italian and Flemish masterpieces. The collectors Lucas van Uffelen and Alfonso Lopez have already been mentioned, in the context of the auction of van Uffelen's art collection in 1639;[18] but Marten Kretzer, Renier van der Wolff and the brothers Gerard and Jan Reynst also owned a larger number of Italian works of art.[19] The Reynst brothers' cabinet in particular contained only Italian art (except for three paintings by the 'Italianized' Dutchman Pieter van Laer), and was unique among the Dutch private collections.[20]

Gerard and Jan Reynst were the sons of Gerrit Reynst, the Amsterdam merchant and founder-member of the *Verenigde Oost-Indische Compagnie* (VOC), who went to the East Indies in 1613 as the Company's second Governor General. Gerard Reynst was a successful merchant and, for a while, was a director of the Wisselbank in Amsterdam. His brother, Jan Reynst, settled in Venice and became a leading participant in the Levantine trade there, where he laid the foundations of a collection – which would later become famous – by buying the collection of cabinet pieces belonging to the Venetian aristocrat Andrea Vendramini. He shipped the collection to Amsterdam and displayed the works of art in his house on the Keizersgracht so that they could be admired by local and foreign visitors alike.

Reynst's collection contained *naturalia* (animals, minerals, fossils) and *artificialia* and thus was a traditional Baroque display of rare specimens. The collection consisted of about 300 sculptures, 10 grave monuments, 5 votive reliefs, 9 urns, 250 vases, innumerable coins as well as the 200 paintings that are of particular interest here. Among these were some outstanding sixteenth-century Venetian masterpieces – they had already been published in a contemporary catalogue – that did not form part of the

Vendramini collection but had been collected individually in Venice and northern Italy. Reynst's collection became internationally famous after his death, not because of its catalogue, the *Caelaturae*, or because of the entries that foreign travellers wrote in the visitors' book, but because twenty-two paintings and twelve antique sculptures from the collection were chosen as an official present for the English King, Charles II, in 1660.[21] The local governments of the provinces of Holland and West Friesland had hoped that the king could help to restore the deteriorating Anglo–Dutch relations – a hope that was to prove to have been misplaced – and, as he set off from Scheveningen to England, they promised him many valuable presents. Among these presents was a state yacht, which was a special gift from the city of Amsterdam, four paintings by Dutch painters – three of them by Gerrit Dou – as well as the treasures from the Reynst brothers' collection.

Jan Reynst died in 1646, and Gerard Reynst drowned in the Keizersgracht in 1658. Therefore, the art dealer Gerrit van Uylenburgh and the sculptor Artus Quellius were commissioned to choose pictures and sculptures worth 80,000 guilders from the collection owned by Gerard Reynst's widow with which to present the king, who preferred the Italian style to the Dutch. The gifts were ceremoniously presented by the ambassadors of the States General in November 1660. According to contemporary sources the king was particularly pleased with the *Mother and Child* attributed to Titian. Apart from this, other paintings in the Reynst collection can be identified with the help of Charles II's inventory, which lists fourteen paintings that are also listed in the printed catalogue of the Reynst collection.[22] There was a Bassano, a Bonifazio Veronese, an alleged Giorgione, a Guercino, two Lottos, a Parmigianino, an alleged Reni, a Giulio Romano, a Tintoretto, three Titians (or paintings from the School of Titian) and a Paolo Veronese; most of these are now in the Royal Collection at Hampton Court and, with paintings like Titian's *Sannazaro*, were the best that the Reynst brothers' cabinet had to offer. Ten years after the gift to Charles II, in 1670, the Reynst collection was sold – it is not known to whom, or for how much. However, part of it must have been acquired by Gerrit van Uylenburgh, who offered it for sale to the Great Elector of Brandenburg in 1671.[23]

He was not as successful in this matter as in his choice of paintings for the English king. Perhaps his offer consisted of pictures of a lower quality than those from the Vendramini collection.

Although nothing is known about the authenticity of the works in the other Amsterdam collections of Italian art, it is reasonable to suppose that a collector like the merchant Marten Kretzer – the leading man on the Amsterdam art scene in the middle of the seventeenth century – was in a position to prove the authenticity of his Titian, Bassano or del Sarto.[24] Marten Kretzer was referred to not only as being an outstanding collector by Houbraken and Sandrart but was also considered to be an expert. For example, he valued the estate of the art dealer Johannes de Renialme, who also had a large stock of Italian paintings. Apart from this, Kretzer supported the founding of a painters' brotherhood in Amsterdam, which was independent of the Guild of St Luke; he was also one of the heads of the theatre there. Apart from the Italian masters, his collection of paintings, was composed of a good cross-section of contemporary good-quality Flemish and Northern Dutch art. As well as the Flemings (Rubens, Jordaens, Willem Key and Floris) and the Dutch Italianists – among them Lastman, Poelenburgh, Pynas, Honthorst, Terbruggen and van Laer – Rembrandt, Lievens, Porcellis, Carel Fabritius and Emanuel de Witte were also widely represented. In contrast, the works of Pieter van den Bosch (whom Kretzer had employed in 1645, at a salary of 1,200 guilders for the year), seem to have been intended for the general market rather than for inclusion in Kretzer's own collection.[25] According to the contract, Pieter van den Bosch was supposed to spend each day painting the pictures that Kretzer proposed. This is an example of a fluid transition from art collecting to dealing.

Special relationships developed between collectors and painters if a painter got into financial difficulties and ended up becoming dependent on the collector. Rembrandt had such a relationship with his *geldschieter* (money-lender), the collector Herman Becker.[26] Herman Becker was probably a member of the Riga merchant class and had been in the Baltic trade since the 1640s; he was soon acting as a merchant-banker in Amsterdam. He was involved in share dealings, investment in real estate and money-lending. Succeeding generations have become interested in him because of the painters and art dealers to whom he lent money, but his clients were also just as likely to belong to the Amsterdam business world.

The first member of the art world to borrow money from Becker was the dealer Johannes de Renialme. De Renialme took out a loan for 1,485 guilders at five per cent interest, which he does not seem to have repaid by his death in 1657. His estate inventory reveals, among other things, three paintings by Jan Lievens and one by Philips Koninck, as well as jewels worth 1,000 guilders, which had been pledged as security. In the 1660s, Rembrandt was in debt to Becker as a result of three loans: 537 guilders borrowed in 1662 at five per cent interest, 450 guilders borrowed against security in March 1664, as well as a promissory note that Becker had bought from another of the painter's creditors. While Rembrandt had, with difficulty, repaid the first two loans by 1668, he still owed Becker 1,082 guilders, which had accumulated on the promissory note. Rembrandt promised to pay off two thirds of it in cash and the other third in drawings and paintings, within six months. It is not known whether this actually happened and he did repay the debt, however, it says a great deal for Becker that he actually bought the majority of the Rembrandts in his collection and did not extort them from the poverty-stricken artist in payment of his debts, as has previously been suggested.[27] Becker also allowed painters and other debtors to use works of art as security, and when he did this he did not take any interest on the loan.[28] Jan Lievens borrowed a total of 400 guilders over the period 1667/8, for which he pledged a *Sacrifice of Abraham* and a *Pyramus and Thisbe* as well as a *Gideon* and an *Andromeda* as security. Becker, the art lover, was also prepared to help other painters who found themselves in financial difficulties. After Lievens, the landscape painters Frederick de Moucheron, Philips Koninck, Domenicus van Tol and Anthony van der Laen also borrowed money from Becker, pledging pictures as security and thus, in the long run, enhanced his art collection.

The collector Willem Six (7,776 guilders) and the dealer Gerrit van Uylenburgh (1,710 guilders) also beat a path to Becker's door in the Keizersgracht requesting large loans. It was quite usual to use works of art as security, people who were not artists also did this because paintings could be used as security for a loan as long as they were not cheap, mass-produced items. For example, the aristocrat and art collector from The Hague Theodore de Liefvelt borrowed 1,400 guilders from Becker in 1674 and 1675 respectively, for which he pledged sixteen paintings. However, unlike the painters, he had to pay five and six per cent interest, and three years later, when Becker died, there were still 850 guilders outstanding on the debt. However, it would be incorrect to conclude that most of Becker's collection was composed of pledges for loans on which people had defaulted. On the contrary, Becker probably had the most important collection of Dutch art of his time and this could not have been put together as a result of a few relatively small loans to a handful of painters.

Becker's collection totalled 231 pictures. The second most important collection was that of the painter Jan van Capelle, totalling 197 paintings, while the gap separating Becker's collection from that of the third most important collector, Gerrit van Uylenburgh, (95 paintings) was even greater. What made Becker's collection unique was its range. A look at the recorded inventory of the Becker collection (which follows) is like walking through the different subjects and schools of seventeenth-century Dutch painting. The subject and painter are recorded for 137 of the works, the rest are defined by their genre. The artists with the largest number of paintings attributed to them are: Rembrandt (fourteen), Jan Lievens the Elder (six), Jan Lievens the Younger (ten), Philips Koninck (seven), Frederick de Moucheron (five) and Rubens (three). As well as this, the Rembrandt set (Lastman and Bol), the Haarlem painters (Brouwer, Jan de Bray, Goltzius, Cornelis van Haarlem) and the Utrecht School (Poelenburgh) are well represented. As far as types of paintings are concerned, there are, for example, landscapes by Bril, van Everdingen, de Vlieger, Porcellis and Jacob van Ruisdael, animal paintings by Potter and a still life by Willem Kalf. Still lifes and genre pictures are often just cursorily mentioned by their motif (vase of flowers, soldiers or pipe smokers). The Italians are described just as summarily and only a *Preaching John* is mentioned by name as *by Pintoret* (Tintoretto?), however the collection was not famous for having contained outstanding works of the Italian Renaissance. On the contrary, what makes Becker's collection special in comparison with the other large collections that have been mentioned, is that he concentrated on contemporary Dutch art, although the French (Claude Lorrain) or the older German painters (Holbein and Dürer) were also to be found in the collection.

The Paintings in Herman Becker's Estate[29]

fol. 283ᵛᵒ

In the front of the house
A still life by W. Calf
A landscape by Paulus Bril
Ditto by Simon de Vlieger
A bush by Jan Lievens
A landscape by the same painter
A Hercules by P. P. Rubens
Ditto by the same painter
A woman's face by Rembrandt van Rijn
Ditto by Philips Koninck
A man's face by Rembrandt – a self-portrait
A standard-bearer by the same Rembrandt
An Italian horse fair
A painting of Three Kings by Lucas van Leyden
A small Italian landscape by Jan Lap
Ditto by Jan Blom

In progress
A man's face by Rembrandt
(*crossed out:* the Dam by Jacob van Ruisdael) pledged

fol. 284 ʳ

(*crossed out:* A shore by the same Ruisdael, pledged)
A landscape by Lievens
A large painting of a few soldiers by Philips Wouwermans
An Italian Last Supper
A Pontius Pilate by Lievens
An Italian painting of Apollo and Pan
A wedding (*crossed out:* by) in the style of Bruegel
A kitchen and some fruit
A portrait of an old man
An Italian painting of gods and goddesses

In the corridor
A small painting of three farmers by Brouwer
Ditto of horsemen by Jan Martszen the Younger
A shepherd and shepherdess with sheep by J. Felpacker
A nude Ceres with some satyrs
A painting of farmers by Helleman
A church with some monks and figures
An oval painting of a woman's face
A small landscape by Herri Bles
An oval landscape painting
A painting of two farmers in the style of Bruegel
Another oval landscape
An Italian painting of two faces
A landscape by Everdingen
A small round landscape
An oval picture of two gentlemen
A round painting of a bagpipe player

fol. 284vo

A landscape by Lievens
A painting of Italian fortune tellers
A fire at night

In the back porch
A landscape in the style of Paulus Bril
A vase of flowers by J. S.
A still life of a silver lamp by Simon Luttickhuijsen
A girl writing
A landscape by Everdingen
An oval painting of a man's face
An old landscape
A scene with armed soldiers and figures
(*crossed out:* A fruit still life by Cornelis Kick) pledged
A still life by S. Hijmes
A picture of the Madonna with other figures by
(*crossed out:* Van Dyck) Rubens
A landscape by Philips Koninck
A picture of tobacco smokers

A Venus and Cupid in the style of Rembrandt
A sacrifice by Jan Lievens the Elder
An Italian painting of a man's face
A large landscape decorated by Teniers
A small man's face in the style of (*crossed out:* Gebra)
    Rembrandt van Rijn
A landscape
A Flight into Egypt
Two backgammon players
A dog by Paulus Potter

fol. 285ʳ

A landscape with figures
Some figures, both singers and players by Steen
A painting in the style of Brouwer

In a room next to the front of the house
A nude Venus with chlidren
A face by Philips Koninck
A woman at a well by Rembrandt van Rijn
(*crossed out:* A girl and a man playing music by Van der
    Burgh) pledged
A life-size Juno
A landscape in a gilded ebony frame
A Crucifixion scene by Rembrandt showing Christ having
    his feet washed
A picture by K. Klabbaert
A woman's face by Holbein with hands
A man's face by de Bray
A woman's face by Ferdinand Bol
A vase of flowers by Hendrick Schoock
A girl drinking
A landscape by Alexander Petit in a gilt frame
A ditto by Ruisdael
A landscape and building with figures by Jan Weenix the
    Elder in a gilt frame
A priest reading a book by Jan Lievens the Elder

A painting of John the Baptist preaching in a gilt frame by
    Pintoret
A partridge and hunting equipment by Guillaume van Aelst
A cliff by Asselijn Krabbetie

fol. 285vo

A nude woman with a philosopher by Bijlert
A large landscape by Jan Lievens the Elder
A meeting of farmers by Philips Koninck painted from life
A fish market by Emanuel de Witte in a gilt frame
A woman's face by de Bray
An Italian man's portrait
A still-life by Simon Luttickhuijsen
A large landscape painting by Jan Bot
A lute player by Jan Lievenszoen the Elder
Some farmers
A still life of a partridge with embellishments
A small coal seller with servant girl
A classical face by Lucas
A Flight into Egypt by
(*crossed out:* the Elder) Weenix
A Zachary and Elisabeth by Schut
A small picture with one nude therein
Figures by Poelenburgh
A sleeping farmer
Some card players
A charlatan
A Three Kings by Rembrandt van Rijn
A portrait by Jan Lievens on the side of the chimney
A painting of Juno, Pallas and Venus in a gilt frame
An old man's face by Lievens the Elder
A large painting of Peace with many embellishments
A Hercules by Mr Cornelis van Haarlem
A Cleopatra by the same painter
A picture of cows
A landscape with gold frame
A sleeping farmer with several other farmers

A small Flight into Egypt by Albrecht Dürer
A horseman by Paulus Potter

fol. 286^r

An Italian Christmas Eve
A hunter by Esaias van de Velde
A storm by Porcellis
A landscape by Poelenburgh with some nude figures,
    among them a woman, who is touching a garlanded goat
A sleeping nude woman with 2 satyrs by Lievens the Elder
A large landscape by Claude Lorrain
Another landscape of the same size
Some riders
A landscape with some figures in the style of Poelenburgh
A Ceres ditto
An old man's face by Ferdinand Bol
A face of a woman with her hand on a chair by Rembrandt
    van Rijn
A Mars and Venus by Goltzius
A still life vanitas by Rembrandt van Rijn
An old man in the style of the same painter
A sea by Porcellis
A David and Jonathan by Rembrandt van Rijn
A still life of gold cup with a rummer
A battle on a rolled up canvas
A still life of a partridge without frame
A portrait of children
A landscape by Herri Bles
A landscape by Schellinks with a gilt frame
Two landscapes by Moucheron
Two larger ditto by the same painter
A landscape with figures in the style of Wouwermans
A fruit still life by the young Weenix
A painting of a man grasping a wine jug and a girl by
    Gabriel Metsu
A lute player in the style of Verburgh
A fruit still life by Breuningh

A girl playing with a dancing dog by Metsu
A landscape with a dancing figure by Jan Lins

fol. 286vo

A panpipes and Pan
(*crossed out:* A woodcut of a coat of arms by Pelgrom.
Added note in the margin in another hand: printed it belongs
   to the children of Gerhard Pelgrom, son of Stephanus
   Pelgrom)

Inside the inner or middle-room
A landscape by van Goor over the door
A calm water with ships
A landscape by Moucheron
A temple or church
A love scene by Barent Graat
A landscape by Mr Govert Jansz
Two old portraits
Two more recent life-size portraits
A kitchen painting
A landscape by Philips Koninck
An Italian painting of three figures
An old landscape painting

In the back room
A Discovery of Moses by Jacob Enas
A sleeping shepherdess and shepherds by Ter Brugge
A singing girl and a viola player by Philips Koninck
A ditto girl leaning over the lower part of a door
A Jeptha in the style of Jacob Pynas
A ditto of nude children in the style of Jan Lievens the
   Elder
A sacrifice by Jan Lievens
A Pallas and (*crossed out:* and Gideon) by Rembrandt van
   Rijn
A Condemnation of Joseph by Potiphar's wife
A bloody rock of Joseph by Jan Lievens
A face by Rembrandt

A kitchen scene
A large painting by Lastman with an ascending angel
A large painting by Hercules Seghers
A ditto baptism of blackamoors by Lastman

In the little room next to the attic storeroom
A hunting equipment still life by Leemans
A landscape by Lievens
Two copies in the style of Lastman, one is a baptism of
  blackamoors and the other an ascending angel
A landscape in the style of Hercules Seghers
A small old painting depicting tobacco on a table

In the front room
A Juno by Rembrandt van Rijn
A Venus and Cupid by the same painter
A Three Kings in the style of Rembrandt
A Three Kings as an altar painting

In the attic storeroom
A hunting equipment still life by Leemans
A life-size Ecce Homo
An old landscape
A large canvas with a sketch by Lievens
The King of Bohemia
The Queen of Bohemia
A shepherdess
An old portrait
A painted weapon

In the bedroom
Three old poor quality pictures

In the room above the corridor
Two portraits
One old portrait
An old school picture
Two old small faces
An Italian painting of Apollo and Pan

fol. 287vo

In the office
A landscape
A painting of a nude woman
A painting of a church
Two ditto without frames of tobacco smokers
A ditto of a woman at a well
A sleeper

Thus far the pictures

Becker's collection was auctioned on 28 March 1679, it is not known how much the individual pictures or indeed the whole collection fetched. It can probably be assumed that it was worth a total of 30–40,000 guilders. This sum was about twenty per cent of Becker's total estate, the value of which was put at 200,000 guilders – 110,000 of which came from promissory notes alone.[30] However, Becker's collection of paintings – he also left 285 books – was an investment that could be capitalized on or used as security.

The seventeenth-century conception of art as an investment has not been adequately researched. Arnold Hauser, who considers the topic in *The Social History of Art*, refers to a quotation from John Evelyn who, in 1641, postulated that since there was an absence of land to invest in, Dutch farmers invested two to three thousand guilders in pictures.[31] Hauser interprets this as meaning that Dutch burghers 'bought pictures, above all, because there was nothing else to buy'.[32] However, the sources do not confirm either Evelyn's statement or Hauser's interpretation: the pictures that were owned by the average Delft household represented only three to ten per cent of the value of their movable assets.[33]

Since the majority of the pictures were in the lower and middle price categories, they did not represent an investment. The investment aspect tended to be significant in speculation in Italian art or in purchasing more expensive fine art. Thus patrons purchased almost all the artistic output from certain artists even before they became famous; then, if the painter was successful, the private collection was sure to increase in value. For example, the first person to collect the Leiden fine artist Gerrit Dou was the Swedish envoy to The Hague, Pieter Spiering. Spiering paid Dou one thousand guilders every year from 1637 and thus ensured the right of first refusal to the artist's work, which he then purchased if he so wished.[34] In doing this, Spiering was investing in an up-and-coming painter and thus taking a certain commercial risk.

In contrast, Johann de Bye from Leiden, who bought Dou from about 1660 onwards, was making a secure investment in purchasing the pictures since the famous master had just declined to accept the position of court painter to Charles II. By 1665, de Bye already owned twenty-nine paintings by Dou, which he exhibited opposite the town hall in Leiden so that he could sell them at a profit.[35] In the case of Johannes Vermeer, it is known that the occasional collector Pieter Claesz. van Ruijven collected Vermeer exclusively and bought at least half the painter's works from 1657 until his death.[36] As was the case with the patrons of Dou and Frans van Mieris, this resulted firstly in turning fine paintings – which could not have been afforded by everyone – into exclusive collectors' items, and secondly in the artists scarcely being represented in the collections of either their home towns or on the Amsterdam art market.

So how can analysing the private art collections help with understanding the function performed by works of art in Dutch households and the taste of the Dutch art buyer? For one thing, the function of works of art or, more particularly, changes in their function, is reflected in the trend away from histories towards landscapes. For another, the difference in the significance placed upon religious subjects in Catholic and Calvinist art collections also points to a change in function. Whereas the Catholics continued to cling to their devotional pictures, the Calvinists accepted religious subjects as, at best, being instructive when they did not just choose their paintings for their own personal enjoyment.

This difference in the collections owned by Catholics and Calvinists shows the change in the function of paintings that took place in microcosm in the Netherlands during the seventeenth century. The devotional function of pictures that dominated throughout the Middle Ages and even into the sixteenth century gave way to an aesthetic function, representing of secularisation in collectors' taste: people bought pictures for their own pleasure and to decorate their houses. As well as the aesthetic function that a landscape or seascape, for example, fulfilled, the instructive aspect of pictures was generally accepted – at least in the first half of the seventeenth century. This is shown by the demand for still lifes and symbolic genre paintings whose beauty was combined with a more or less overt message (vanitas).

Sociologists of taste can now classify certain social groups as having particularly marked differences in artistic taste, but the same cannot be done for the seventeenth century. The inventories of the various income groups show a general common trend; suggesting that all collectors had similar taste, independent of their social status. Apart from a few important collectors, the Dutch bought a certain genre when they could afford it, the choice of a specific painter came second. The number and quality of pictures in a house increased with the occupant's income, but there was no significant change in taste. More prosperous collectors naturally followed the market trends sooner than the ordinary buyer. However, this seems to have been the only difference between the buying habits of these two types of collectors. Therefore the conclusion that trends in art depended on social class cannot be made, but this does not mean that all classes in the Netherlands liked the same kind of art. Some members of the urban élite distanced themselves from the general trend, for example, by collecting Venetian pictures or by subscribing to the works of certain expensive fine painters. Unfortunately, it is impossible to establish how representative such people were, nor can it be said with any certainty who was responsible for dictating the artistic trends.

Contemporary writers on art such as Karel van Mander, Samuel van Hoogstraeten or Gérard de Lairesse should, however, be considered; in their theoretical treatment they addressed themselves not only to the painters but also to a wider public, whom they were trying to bring nearer to the 'high school of the art of painting' – that is, above all, history painting. Although van Mander mentioned certain collectors as connoisseurs and patrons of art,[37] the practical success of his endeavours was to remain limited. The vast majority of collectors bought landscapes, still lifes and genre paintings instead of histories. Even the painters themselves do not seem to have taken much notice of the authors, in the almost two hundred artistic inventories that Bredius published, van Mander appeared only twelve times.[38] It is not known how often he was represented in the collectors' libraries, but it is of note that van Mander's *Schilder-Boek* (Painting Book) was not to be found in the comprehensive library of the important collector Herman Becker.[39] Occasionally the art dealers seem to have influenced the buyers' taste more than those theorizing about art, especially when the increase in the popularity of the older masters is compared with that of contemporary art towards the end of the seventeenth century.

In all, it seems that the private demand for works of art, based on what is known of the collections, was influenced by two main factors. One was the amount of money that the collector had at his disposal, and the other, the way in which the function of the works of art in his house had changed. Since buyers were no longer attached exclusively to devotional pictures, and were looking for something to decorate their rooms instead, they chose the genre that they could afford. In this way, the change in the function of paintings led ultimately to landscapes – whose increasingly short production time made them more and more reasonably priced – dominating art collections.

Conclusion

Two phenomena appear again and again in the study of the Dutch economy, society and painting: commercialization and innovation. These are what shaped the special features of the Netherlands and characterized this society in early modern Europe.

To begin with commercialization shall be examined, which encompassed social relationships as well as agriculture and artistic production. As a result of the gradual relaxation of the strictures of a society based on privilege, the social status of the urban and rural populations was defined more by democratic market-based relationships, which had replaced feudal relationships in the cities and countryside. This meant that agriculture and the rural workers were no longer constrained by the feudal means of production, that is, the lords of the manor could no longer take the lion's share of the farmers' production. Urbanization resulted in agrarian production being controlled by the laws of supply and demand alone. A person's ability to work had become a marketable commodity which could be offered for sale throughout the country. In the cities the distinct status of the upper class was no longer intrinsically important, since a person's social position was now determined by income and wealth. Thus the sumptuary and dress regulations, which were common in olden day Europe, did not exist in the Netherlands. However, this does not mean that Dutch society was socially mobile and open. Political offices, for example, continued to be filled by a small élite, nevertheless this class does not appear to have been hermetically sealed – it was quite possible to advance socially by making a good match.

Market forces had at least as much of an impact on artistic production as they did on agriculture and social relationships.

Paintings were marketable goods which competed for the attention of the purchaser; the prerequisite for this development was the fact that the relationship between the patron and the artist, which had traditionally dominated the art world, had either lost much of its power or had disappeared altogether, hence this corporate barrier no longer controlled the number of paintings that were produced. Thus, even though the Guilds of St Luke were able to determine the way in which painters were educated and trained, and how they auctioned and sold their pictures, the guilds were not, in the long run, in a position to restrict artistic production itself or the import of art. Although it is true that the guilds in centres such as Amsterdam had only a limited influence on the painter's creative endeavours anyway, in smaller cities they seemed flexible enough to have been able to adapt to the needs of the expanding market.

The other phenomenon that made its mark on many areas, especially on the commercial world, was innovation. It does not matter whether one examines horticulture and herring fishing in the primary sector, shipbuilding and cloth dyeing in the industrial or secondary sector, or the new organizational forms like the joint-stock company in the tertiary sector – innovations in production, processing and marketing meant that the Netherlands was able to offer both domestic and foreign mass-produced and luxury goods at low prices. This gave the Dutch a commercial advantage at home and abroad, the result of which was that what had been luxury products became everyday items.

Art was also a part of this innovative climate. The invention of tonal painting made the new landscapes which were painted in this style much cheaper to produce, making the secularized demand for non-religious subjects possible on a grand scale. However, although art, the economy and society in general show clear parallels in terms of commercialization and innovation, it is difficult to categorize the direct influences that were exerted by the economy and society on art.

Such things are, in fact, inherently difficult to prove, but the possible interactions between art and the economy are easier to examine than, for example, the influences of bourgeois society on artistic development. Analysing the relationship between the economy and art does not revolve around the question of whether the booming economy facilitated or hindered investment in art, as suggested by the Lopez Thesis,[1] or whether the Dutch invested money in art because they had no other ways of investing their money. Compared with the amount of money invested in the expanding Dutch economy, investments in the artistic sector were as limited as the relative value of art in the Dutch households – paintings were seldom worth more than about three per cent of the inventory of movable goods.

More interesting, however, is the connection between economic growth, an increase in prosperity and the private demand for works of art. In the Netherlands, for the first time in European history, the middle classes also demanded works of art; this had the effect of encouraging a more wide-ranging art as well as producing numerous artistic achievements of a very high quality. The prerequisite for this increase in demand, which not only encompassed works of art but also furnishing articles of every kind, was the prosperity of the purchasers which, in turn, can easily be linked to the Netherlands' economic growth. Private individuals maintained their level of prosperity even towards the end of the seventeenth century, despite the stagnation of the Dutch economy; in fact, at around the same time, the Dutch per capita income, which was the highest in the Europe, continued to increase.

Changes in the choice of subject-matter paralleled the increased demand for art. The purchasers preferred genre painting and subjects that they understood and could afford. Thus the allegorical and mythological subjects, which required a certain level of education, were no longer popular on the art market, and the more expensive histories were replaced by cheap landscapes. However, this could happen only as a result of the influence of Calvinism, that had given art a new ideological basis by stimulating the changes that led to art having an aesthetic function instead of being used solely as a focus for devotion.

The private ownership of pictures and the demands of the art market, which were reflected in the increasing popularity of landscapes, introduced a certain secularization. Religious paintings were rarely displayed, moralizing and instructive messages were now contained in still lifes and genre pictures, which meant that, in turn, the instructive and moralizing aspect of art gradually

21   Willem Claesz Heda, *Breakfast Table with Bacon*, 1646, Schwerin,
Staatliches Museum.

diminished. Still lifes were replaced by genre paintings, the
significance of which gradually vanished. This gradual erosion
of the paintings' underlying meanings, following the expansion
of the market, is worthy of study by iconologists;[2] who might
demonstrate a way out of the realism-surface realism (*realisme-
schijnrealisme*) debate. Even the sociology of art thesis, which
describes the bourgeois preference for Realism, would appear in
a new light. The bourgeoisie, however defined, did not in fact
always prefer realistic art. The prerequisites governing this change
in subject-matter were, on the one hand, an effect of Calvinism
and the new function that works of art had acquired, and on the
other, due to the fact that those who purchased art came from
different social classes and no longer easily comprehended
mythology, allegory or even the hidden messages in still lifes and
genre paintings.

The connection between the economic boom, a growing prosperity and an expanding demand for works of art, which influenced the trends in the art market, can be seen very clearly. But what did it look like towards the end of the seventeenth century as the Dutch economy stagnated at a high level? It would be facile to link the stagnation of the economy directly with developments in art by pointing to the reduction in wealth, and thus to a more limited market. There are no indications that suggest a reduction in prosperity in the seventeenth century, even though, towards the end of the century, a great deal of the wealth was concentrated in the hands of the rich. The per capita income continued to increase, and the reduction in the price of grain freed a portion of people's income to be used for other consumer goods.

However, there are certain parallels between developments in the economy and the art market. The market may be described as being saturated, whether one refers to Dutch industrial products or Dutch art. In contrast to the period of growth in the 1630s, few collections of contemporary art were compiled in the 1680s and 90s – when there was a lack of growth in both the economy and the population. When people bought art, they preferred to purchase the more expensive paintings by the old masters, thus undermining the domestic art market; just as the Dutch consumers' preference for foreign products had a detrimental effect on domestic industry. The number of painters working in the market shrank, especially in the small and medium-sized cities; as did the number of Dutch people working in industry. The diversity in artistic production was lost, and innovation no longer played an important role in either the domestic or the foreign markets.

By attempting finally to define the characteristics that made Dutch painting in the seventeenth century unique, one is confronted with comparisons with the Italian Renaissance. In fact, research into the Italian Renaissance has greatly influenced the way in which seventeenth-century Dutch art is interpreted. Fifteenth and sixteenth-century Italy saw the birth of many phenomena which, 100 to 150 years later, were to be fully developed in the Netherlands. For example, in Northern Italy, fifteenth-century clients had begun to buy works of art as finished products, and merchants were beginning to specialize in art dealing.[3] Despite the fact that these dealers' clients came almost exclusively from the princely Renaissance courts, it is known that paintings were also exhibited at fairs. However, patronage and the commissioning of works of art continued to remain the dominant market factors, since a wider demand for works of art did not develop. Thus it was the patrons and the clients who supported the new artistic developments during the Renaissance.

The start of the secularization of artistic taste may also be traced right back to the late Renaissance. Thus, Peter Burke, based on I. Errera's *Répertoire des peintures datées*, noted the increasing proportion of secular subjects in paintings between 1480 and 1539.[4]

Table 7 Secular subject-matter 1480–1539	
Period	Secular subject-matter as a % of art produced
1480–89	5
1490–99	9
1500–09	10
1510–19	11
1520–29	13
1530–39	22

Even if the number of paintings that have survived is not representative of the work that was produced and collected in the Renaissance, the increasing aesthetic function of works of art was becoming obvious. This change in the function of art first found its fulfilment in Calvinist Holland, where the proportion of secular subjects at the beginning of the seventeenth century already stood at about sixty-five per cent and, by the end of the century, had reached approximately ninety per cent.

A further similarity between the Dutch Golden Age and the Italian Renaissance was the fact that neither of these eras was able to carry its innovations and modernity into another age, and each went out of fashion very suddenly. In Italy, this has been traced back to the Florentine families' retreat from trade, and an increase in the number of men with private incomes. This development was accompanied by a change in values – crafts were not valued very highly – and though in the short term this promised more commissions from the feudalized merchants, in the long term it led to a reduction in the spirit of competition and innovation.[5]

Competition and innovation among the painters were also closely linked in seventeenth-century Dutch painting. In contrast with the Renaissance, however, Dutch painters were not supported by a few well-to-do clients but were reliant upon a broader clientele. Innovation came to a standstill only when the market for contemporary art was saturated and the *nouveaux riches* began to demand old masters, expensive fine paintings or even Italian paintings, at the same time as the wide range of artworks began to diminish. This meant that the exchange of ideas between artistic centres and the mobility of the artists lessened – even in a country as densely populated as the Netherlands. The people also seem to have been less mobile.[6] Artistic production stagnated above all in small cities, even though the population continued to benefit from the economic, social and cultural achievements of the Golden Age for a long time.

Notes

I HISTORICAL INTERPRETATIONS

1 G. W. F. Hegel, *Ästhetik*, ed. F. Bassenge, Berlin 1955, 803–804.

2 P. Demetz, 'Defenses of Dutch Painting and the Theory of Realism', *Comparative Literature* 15, no. 2 (1963), 111. On Hegel and the reception of Dutch painting see also J. Bialostocki, 'Einfache Nachahmung der Natur oder symbolische Weltschau. Zu den Deutungsproblemen der holländischen Malerei des 17. Jhdt.', *Zeitschrift für Kunstgeschichte 47*, (1984), 421–38.

3 S. van Hoogstraeten, *Inleyding tot de Hooge Schoole der Schilder-konst*, Rotterdam 1678, 25. Trans. from *Die Sprache der Bilder*, exh. cat., Braunschweig 1978, 11. The original quotation is: '. . . *een volmaekte Schildery is als een spiegel van de Natuer, die de dingen, die niet en zijn, doet schijnen te zijn, en op een geoorlofde vermakelijke en prijslijke wijze bedriegt'*.

4 Bialostocki, 'Einfache Nachahmung', 422.

5 Demetz, 'Defenses', 97–8.

6 W. *Bürgers* (pseudonym of Thoré), *Kunstkritik*, rev. A. Schmarsow, and B. Klemm, Leipzig 1908, 26 (trans. from French).

7 P. Hecht, 'The Debate on Symbol and Meaning in Dutch Seventeenth Century Art: An Appeal to Common Sense', *Simiolus* 16 (1986), 175.

8 E. Fromentin, *Die Alten Meister (Belgien-Holland)*, Potsdam 1919, 169 (trans. from French).

9 F. G. Hotho, *Geschichte der deutschen und niederländischen Malerei*, I, Berlin 1842, 48, 58, 137; Demetz, 'Defenses', 103.

10 See, for example, A. Riegl, *Das holländische Gruppenporträt*, Vienna 1931.

11 A. Warburg, 'Sandro Botticelli's "Geburt der Venus" und "Frühling". Eine Untersuchung über die Vorstellungen von der Antike in der italienischen Frührenaissance', Hamburg–Leipzig 1893, rep. in id., *Gesammelte Schriften*, I, Leipzig–Berlin 1932, 1–59, 307–28. For further details about reception see K. Renger, 'Zur Forschungsgeschichte der Bilddeutung in der holländischen Malerei', in *Die Sprache der Bilder*, exh. cat., Braunschweig 1978, 34–8.

12 E. Panofsky, 'Der gefesselte Eros (Zur Genealogie von Rembrandts Danae)', *Oud Holland 50* (1933), 193–217.

13 H. Kauffmann 'Die Fünfsinne in der niederländischen Malerei des 17. Jahrhunderts', in *Festschrift Dagobert Frey*, Breslau 1943, 135–57. H. Rudolph, ' "Vanitas". Die Bedeutung mittelalterlicher und humanistischer Bildinhalte in der niederländischen Malerei des 17. Jahrhunderts', in *Festschrift Wilhelm Pinder*, Leipzig 1938, 405–33.

14 S. Gudlaugsson, *Ikonographische Studien über die holländische Malerei und das Theater des 17. Jahrhunderts*, Würzburg 1938; id., *Komedianten bij Jan Steen en zijn tijdgenoten*, The Hague 1945.

15 J. Huizinga, *Holländische Kultur im*

siebzehnten Jahrhundert, Basel 1961, 112–13.

16 I. Bergström, *Dutch Still-Life Painting in the Seventeenth Century*, London 1956.

17 Cited in R. Raben, and R. Vermeij, 'Worteloof en Cultuurhistorie. Kunstopvattingen van Peter Hecht en Eddy de Jongh', *Leidschrift* 6, no. 3 (1990), 51. See also, *Tot lering en vermaak. Betekenissen van Hollandse genrevoorstellingen uit de zeventiende eeuw*, exh. cat., Amsterdam 1976.

18 Roemer Visscher, the author of a book on emblems which appeared in 1641 defined *sinnepop* as 'a short, pithy utterance which at first glance cannot be understood by every Tom, Dick, and Harry, yet is not so obscure that, by guessing, one may not hit yea or nay nevertheless, some reflection and deliberation are required in order to savor the sweetness of the kernel or pill' cited in B. Haak, *The Golden Age: Dutch Painters of the Seventeenth Century*, translated from the Dutch and edited by E. Willems-Treeman, London 1984, 73.

19 E. de Jongh, 'Erotica in vogelperspectief. De dubbelzinnigheid van een reeks 17de eeuwse genrevoorstellingen', *Simiolus* 3 (1968/9), 22–74.

20 E. J. Sluijter, 'Hoe realistisch is de Noordnederlandse schilderkunst van de zeventiende eeuw? De problemen van een vraagstelling', *Leidschrift* 6, no. 3 (1990), 6–14; id., 'Schilders van "cleyne, subtile ende curieuze dingen". Leidse "fijnschilders" in contemporaine bronnen', in E. J. Sluijter et al. (eds), *Leidse fijnschilders*, exh. cat., Leiden 1988, Zwolle–Leiden 1988, 15–55.

21 Ibid., 25–7.

22 S. Alpers, *The Art of Describing: Dutch Art in the Seventeenth Century*, Chicago–London, 1983.

23 Ibid.

24 E. H. Gombrich, 'The Social History of Art', in id., *Meditations on a Hobby Horse and other Essays on the Theory of Art*, London–New York 1978, 86,

(originally appeared in a review of the 1951 English edition of A. Hauser's, *Sozialgeschichte der Kunst und Literatur*.

25 A. von Martin, *Sociology of the Renaissance* (London 1944), New York 1967.

26 F. Antal, *Florentine Painting and its Social Background*, London 1947.

27 Cited in A. Esch, 'Über den Zusammenhang von Kunst und Wirtschaft in der italienischen Renaissance. Ein Forschungsbericht', *Zeitschrift für Historische Forschung* 8 (1981), 187.

28 V.-L. Tapié, *Baroque et classicisme*, Paris 1957; id., 'Baroque et classisime', *Annales: Economies-Sociétés-Civilisations* 14 (1959), 719–31.

29 A. Hauser, *The Social History of Art*, vol. II: *Renaissance, Mannerism, Baroque*, translated in collaboration with the author by Stanley Godman, London, 1962; reprinted 1992, 11–12.

30 Ibid., 193.

31 Ibid., 194.

32 Š. M. Rosenthal, 'O nekotorych social'nych predposylkach gollandskoj I flamanskoj živopisi XVII veka. Predvaritelnye materialy k sociologičeskomu izučeniju iskusstva', *Pamjatnike gosudarstvennogo muzeja izjaščych iskusstv* 5 (1926), 91–108.

33 J. M. Montias 'Socio-Economic Aspects of Netherlandisch Art from the Fifteenth to the Seventeenth Century: A Survey', *Art Bulletin* 72 (1990), 364.

34 E. Larsen (with the collaboration of J. Davidson), *Calvinist Economy and 17th Century Dutch Art*, Lawrence, Kansas, 1979, 59.

35 Ibid., 59.

36 Ibid., 61.

37 F. van Heek, 'Bloie en ondergang van de Hollandse zeventiende-eeuwse landschapsschilderkunst (1620–1670). Artistiek isolement – integratie – creativiteit. Een sociologische beschouwing', *Mens en maatschappij*, no. 2 (1979), 127–43.

38 J. L. Price, *Culture and Society in the Dutch Republic during the 17th Century*, London 1974, 119–69.

39 Gombrich, 'Social History', 86.

40 P. Burke, *Culture and Society in Renaissance Italy 1420–1540*, London 1972.

41 Ibid., 292.

42 M. Wackernagel, *Der Lebensraum des Künstlers in der florentinischen Renaissance*, Leipzig 1938. Instead of 'milieu' Wackernagel used the expression 'Lebensraum', a term that has now become obsolete in this context. English translation *The World of the Florentine Renaissance Artist*, Princeton 1981.

43 Å. Bengtsson, *Studies on the Rise of Realistic Painting in Holland 1610–1625*, Stockholm 1952.

44 L. A. Stone-Ferrier, *Images of Textiles: The Weave of Seventeenth-Century Dutch Art and Society*, Ann Arbor 1980.

45 J. M. Montias, *Artists and Artisans in Delft: A Socio-Economic Study of the Seventeenth Century*, Princeton 1982; id., *Vermeer and his Milieu: A Web of Social History*, Princeton 1988.

46 C. Burney, *A General history of Music*, 4 vols, London 1776–89, II, 584; cited in Burke, *Renaissance*, London 1974, 5.

47 R. S. Lopez, 'Hard Times and Investment in Culture', in *The Renaissance: Six Essays*, New York 1962, 29–54.

48 Esch, 'Zusammenhang', 221.

49 Ibid., 219.

50 J. H. Munro, 'Economic Depression and the Arts in the Fifteenth-Century Low Countries', *Renaissance and Reformation* 19 (1983), 235–50.

51 A. C. van Oss and B. H. Slicher van Bath, 'An Experiment in the History of Economy and Culture', *Journal of European Economic History* 7 (1978), 407–14.

52 W. Brulez, *Cultuur en getal. Aspecten van de relatie economie-maatschappij-cultuur in Europa tussen 1400 en 1800*, Amsterdam 1986.

53 Ibid., 83.

II THE DUTCH ECONOMY

1 D. Defoe, *A Plan of the English Commerce*, London 1728, 192, cited in C. Wilson, 'The Decline of the Netherlands', in *Economic History and the Historian. Collected Essays*, London 1969, 22.

2 W. Temple, *Observations upon the United Provinces of the Netherlands*, ed. George Clark, Oxford 1972, 109.

3 George Downing in a letter to Clarendon 8 July 1661, cited in C. Wilson, *Profit and Power: A Study of England and the Dutch Wars*, London 1957, 3.

4 Compiled from J. Riley, 'The Dutch Economy After 1650: Decline or Growth?', *Journal of European Economic History* 13 (1984), 531.

5 J. de Vries, *The Dutch Rural Economy in the Golden Age, 1500–1700*, New Haven–London, 1974, 87.

6 J. van Houtte, 'Het economische verhal van het Zuiden', *Algemene Geschiedenis der Nederlanden*, V, Utrecht 1952, 184–6.

7 De Vries, *Rural Economy*, 111.

8 Ibid., 115.

9 Ibid., 172.

10 Ibid., 153–4.

11 J. Bouman, *Bedijking, opkomst en bloei van de Beemster*, Amsterdam 1857, 267; De Vries, *Rural Economy*, 192–6.

12 W. Abel, *Agrarkrisen und Agrarkonjunktur. Eine Geschichte der Land- und Ernährungswirtschaft Mitteleuropas seit dem hohen Mittelalter*, Hamburg–Berlin 1966, 142–4, 152–72.

13 R. W. Unger, 'Dutch Herring, Technology and International Trade in the Seventeenth Century', *Journal of Economic History* 40 (1980), 253.

14 Ibid., 257.

15 Ibid., 261.

16 Ibid., 279.

17 J. R. Bruijn, and C. A. Davids, 'Jonas vrij. De nederlandse Walvisvaart, in het bijzonder de Amsterdamse, in de jaren 1640–1644', *Economisch- en sociaal-historisch jaarboek* 38 (1975), 141–78.

18 J. L. van Zanden, 'De economie van Holland in de periode 1650–1805:

groei of achteruitgang? Een overzicht van bronnen, problemen en
resultaten', *Bijdragen en mededelingen
betreffende de Geschiedenis der Nederlanden* 102 (1987), 603.

19 Based on N. W. Postumus, *De
geschiedenis van de Leidsche lakenindustrie*, 3 vols (The Hague 1908)
1939.

20 C. Wilson, *England's Apprenticeship,
1603–1763*, London 1965, 71.

21 B. E. Supple, *Commercial Crisis and
Change in England 1600–42*, Cambridge 1959, 34.

22 Postumus, *Geschiedenis*, III, 930–2,
941–4, 1098–101.

23 P. Kriedte, *Spätfeudalismus und Handelskapital. Grundlinien der europäischen Wirtschaftsgeschichte vom 16. bis
zum Ausgang des 18. Jahrhunderts*,
Göttingen 1980, 91.

24 R. W. Unger, *Dutch Shipbuilding
before 1800. Ships and Guilds*, Assen–
Amsterdam 1978, 36.

25 Ibid., 116–17.

26 P. W. Klein, 'De zeventiende eeuw',
in J. H. van Stuijvenberg (ed.), *De
economische geschiedenis van Nederland*, Groningen 1977, 98.

27 De Vries, *Rural Economy*, 240–1.

28 J. de Vries, 'An Inquiry into the
Behaviour of Wages in the Dutch
Republic and the Southern Nether-
lands from 1580 to 1800', in M.
Aymard (ed.), *Dutch Capitalism and
World Capitalism*, Cambridge–Paris
1982, 46–8.

29 J. de Vries, *De economische achteruitgang der Republiek in de achttiende
eeuw*, Amsterdam 1959, 98–104.

30 Van Zanden, 'Economie', 605.

31 Wilson, *Profit*, 111.

32 J. I. Israel, *Dutch Primacy in World
Trade, 1585–1740*, Oxford 1989,
21–2.

33 An overview of the sixteenth century
can be found in M. North,
*Geldumlauf und Wirtschaftskonjunktur
im südlichen Ostseeraum an der Wende
zur Neuzeit (1440–1570)*, Sigmaringen 1990, 139–41; see also the
seminal work by A. E. Christensen,
Dutch Trade to the Baltic around 1600,
Copenhagen–The Hague 1941.

34 Israel, *Primacy*, 143.

35 J. A. Faber, 'The Decline of the
Baltic Grain-Trade in the Second
Half of the Seventeenth Century',
Acta Historiae Neerlandica 1 (1968),
108–31; see also M. North and F. S
napper, 'The Baltic Trade and the
Decline of the Dutch Economy in
the 18th Century', in J. P. S.
Lemmink, and J. S. van Koningsbrugge (eds), *Baltic Affairs. Relations
between the Netherlands and North-
Eastern Europe*, Nijmegen 1990, 263–
86.

36 Israel, *Primacy*, 55.

37 Ibid., 307–13.

38 W. S. Unger, 'Nieuwe gegevens
betreffende het begin der vaart
op Guinea', *Economisch-historisch
jaarboek* 21 (1940), 194–217.

39 N.-H. Schneeloch, *Aktionäre der
Westindischen Compagnie von 1674.
Die Verschmelzung der alten Kapitalgebergruppen zu einer neuen Aktiengesellschaft*, Stuttgart 1982, 17–22.

40 C. R. Boxer, *The Dutch in Brazil,
1624–1625*, (Oxford 1957), Camden
1973.

41 Israel, *Primacy* , 320–4.

42 While the annual gold imports from
Guinea in 1680s were still running at
about 500,000–600,000 guilders,
after 1697 they had fallen to only
200,000–300,000 guilders, see N.-H.
Schneeloch, 'Die Bewindhebber der
Westindischen Compagnie in der
Kammer Amsterdam, 1674–1700',
*Economisch- en sociaal-historisch jaar-
boek* 36 (1973), 71.

43 F. S. Gaastra, 'Die Vereinigte
Ostindische Compagnie der Niederlande', in E. Schmitt et al. (eds),
*Kaufleute als Kolonialherren: Die
Handelswelt der Niederländer vom Kap
der Guten Hoffnung bis Nagasaki
1600–1800*, Bamberg 1988, 3–7.

44 Ibid., pp. 7–12; W. Reinhard,
*Geschichte der europäischen Expansion,
I: Die Alte Welt bis 1818*, Stuttgart–
Berlin–Cologne–Mainz 1983, 114.

45 K. Glamann, *Dutch–Asiatic Trade
1620–1740*, Copenhagen–The Hague
1958, 12–21, especially 14 (Table
2).

46 I. Schöffer, and F. S. Gaastra, 'The
    Import of Bullion and Coin into
    Asia by the Dutch East India Com-
    pany in the Seventeenth and Eight-
    eenth Centuries', in M. Aymard
    (ed.) *Dutch Capitalism and World
    Capitalism*, Cambridge–Paris 1982,
    215–33; Gaastra, 'Compagnie', 89
    (Table 13).

47 Gaastra, 'Compagnie', 55.

48 Here based on Wilson, *Profit*.

49 Klein, 'Seventiende eeuw', 106–08.

50 H. van der Wee, 'Monetary Credit
    and Banking Systems', in E. E. Rich,
    and C. Wilson (eds), *The Cambridge
    Economic History of Europe. V: The Eco-
    nomic Organization of Early Modern
    Europe*, Cambridge 1977, 337–42;
    J. G. van Dillen, 'La Banque de
    changes et les banquiers privés à
    Amsterdam aux XVIIe et XVIIIe
    siècles', *Third International Conference
    of Economic History, Munich 1965*, V,
    Paris 1974, 177–85.

51 Van der Wee, 'Monetary Systems',
    343–6.

52 For information on the level of sav-
    ings in eighteenth century see J. C.
    Riley, *International Government
    Finance and the Amsterdam Capital
    Market 1740–1815*, Cambridge 1980,
    11–13.

53 J. de Vries, *Economy of Europe in an
    Age of Crisis*, Cambridge 1976, 211–
    12; P. W. Klein, 'Stagnation écono-
    mique et emploi du capital dans la
    Hollande des XVIIIe et XIXe
    siècles', *Revue du Nord* 52 (1970), no.
    204, 38.

54 Contemporaries such as the Gov-
    ernor of the English East India
    Company, Josiah Child, already
    knew that the superiority of the
    Dutch trade was founded on the
    low rates of interest, Israel, *Primacy*,
    413.

III Dutch Society

 1 K. Bosl, and H. Mommsen, 'Adel',
    *Sowjetsystem und Demokratische Gesell-
    schaft*, I, Freiburg 1966, 51.

 2 J. de Vries, *The Dutch Rural Economy

    in the Golden Age, 1500–1700*, New-
    Haven–London, 1974, 35–6.

 3 H. F. K. van Nierop, *Van ridders tot
    regenten*, Dieren 1984, 247–53.

 4 De Vries, *Rural Economy*, 211.

 5 Ibid., 211.

 6 Ibid., 55. Compare above p. 22–3.

 7 W. Abel, *Agrarkrisen und Agrarkon-
    junktur. Eine Geschichte der Land- und
    Ernährungswirtschaft Mitteleuropas seit
    dem hohen Mittelalter*, Hamburg–
    Berlin 1966, 151–72.

 8 A. T. van Deursen, *Het Kopergeld
    van de Gouden eeuw*, I: Het dagelijks
    brood, Assen–Amsterdam, 28; De
    Vries, *Rural Economy*, 184.

 9 P. de la Court, 'Interest van Holland
    ofte gronden van Hollands wel-
    varen, Amsterdam 1661', 38, cited in
    De Vries, *Rural Economy*, 184.

10 De Vries, *Rural Economy*, 216–24.

11 Ibid., 222.

12 Cornelis Jacobs Maals, who has
    already been mentioned, left 279
    guilders as a share in a wooden ship,
    800 guilders in two annuity bonds at
    3.5 per cent interest, 150 guilders as
    a loan at 4 per cent interest and a
    provincial loan over 1,000 guilders.

13 G. Groenhuis, *De Predikanten. De
    sociale positie van de gereformeerde
    predikanten in de Republik der Verenigde
    Nederlanden voor ± 1700*, Groningen
    1977, 45.

14 G. J. Renier, *De Noord-Nederlandse
    Natie*, Utrecht 1948, 115–18.

15 D. J. Roorda, *Partij en Factie. De
    oproeren van 1672 in de steden van
    Holland en Zeeland. Een krachtmeting
    tussen partijen en facties*, Groningen
    1961, 39–58.

16 Groenhuis, *Predikanten*, 64–5.

17 Cited in Groenhuis, *Predikanten*, 66.

18 H. van Dijk, and D. J. Roorda,
    'Sociale mobiliteit onder regenten
    van de Republiek', *Tijdschrift voor
    Geschiedenis* 84 (1971), 306–28.

19 J. A. Faber, *Drie Eeuwen Friesland.
    Economische en sociale ontwikkelingen
    van 1500 tot 1800*, II, Wageningen
    1972, 530–1 (Table VI, 34).

20 Groenhuis, *Predikanten*, 48; in 1668
    de Witt's salary was doubled to 6,000
    guilders.

21 J. de Vries, *Barges and Capitalism:
    Passenger Transportation in the Dutch
    Economy, 1632–1839,* Utrecht 1981,
    134; id., 'An Inquiry into the Behav-
    iour of Wages in the Dutch Republic
    and the Southern Netherlands from
    1580 to 1800', in M. Aymard (ed.),
    *Dutch Capitalism and World Capital-
    ism,* Cambridge–Paris 1982, 40–3;
    Riley, 'The Dutch Economy After
    1650: Decline or Growth?', *Journal of
    European Economic History* 13 (1984),
    538.
22 Van Deursen, *Kopergeld,* I, 53; see
    also J. L. van Zanden, *The Rise and
    Decline of Holland's Economy: Merchant
    Capitalism and the Labour Market,*
    Manchester 1993, 62–3.
23 De Vries, 'Behaviour', 50–51. Cri-
    tical comment on this in J. L.
    van Zanden, *Arbeid tijdens het
    handelskapitalisme,* Bergen 1991,
    172–3.
24 Van Deursen, *Kopergeld,* I, 80.
25 Ibid., 73.
26 G. King, *Two Tracts: Natural and
    Political Observations and Conclusions
    upon the State and Condition of
    England,* ed. G.E. Barnett, Baltimore
    1936, 55. The opinions on how one
    should quantify the value that was
    estimated by King vary greatly. They
    range from 100 guilders (Klein), to
    125 guilders (Riley) and 150 guil-
    ders (Maddison) up to 200 guilders
    (De Vries); Klein, 'De Zeventiende
    eeuw', in J.H. van Stuijvenberg
    (ed.), *De economische geschiedenis
    van Nederland,* Groningen 1977,
    80–1; Riley, 'Dutch Economy', 538;
    A. Maddison, *Groeifasen van het
    kapitalisme,* Utrecht–Antwerp 1982,
    239–41; J. de Vries, 'The Decline
    and Rise of the Dutch Economy,
    1675–1900', in G. Saxonhouse, and
    G. Wright (eds), *Technique, Spirit,
    and Form in the Making of the Modern
    Economics: Essays in the Honour of
    William N. Parker,* Greenwich 1984,
    168.
27 De Vries, 'Economie', 213.
28 P. W. Klein, 'De heffing van de 100e
    en 200e penning van het vermogen
    te Gouda, 1599–1722', *Economisch-*

historisch jaarboek 31 (1965/6), 47–
53.
29 H. van der Wee, 'De economie als
    factor bij het begin van de opstand
    in de Zuidelijke Nederlanden',
    *Bijdragen en mededelingen betreffende
    de geschiedenis der Nederlanden* 83
    (1969), 31.
30 Van Dijk, Roorda, 'Mobiliteit', 306–
    28.
31 Based on P. W. Klein, *De Trippen
    in de 17e eeuw. Een studie over het
    ondernemersgedrag op de Hollandse
    stapelmarkt,* Assen 1965.
32 P. Burke, *Venice and Amsterdam. A
    Study of Seventeenth-Century Élites,*
    London 1974, 112.
33 Ibid., 106.

Aristocratisation in Amsterdam families 1618–1702		
Period	% without an occupation	% with a country house
1618–50	33	10
1650–72	66	41
1672–1702	55	30
1702	48	81

34 Ibid., 10.
35 Groenhuis, *Predikanten,* 54–61.
36 Ibid., 56.
37 Ibid., 58–9.
38 Van Deursen, *Kopergeld,* I, 91.
39 It is now almost impossible to
    acquire an overview on this topic.
    A research perspective can be
    found in V. Press, 'Französische
    Volkserhebungen und deutsche
    Agrarkonflikte zwischen dem 16.
    und dem 18. Jahrhundert', *Beiträge
    zur historischen Sozialkunde* 7 (1977),
    76–81, and P. Blickle, *Unruhen in der
    ständischen Gesellschaft 1300–1800,*
    Munich 1988.
40 R. Dekker, *Holland in beroering.
    Oproeren in de 17de en 18de eeuw,*
    Baarn 1982, 41–5.
41 For the political background see
    H. Lademacher, *Geschichte der Nie-
    derlande. Politik-Verfassung-Wirtschaft,*
    Darmstadt 1983, 104–09, 117–21,
    172–81.

42 Dekker, *Holland*, 23–8.
43 Ibid., 28–38.
44 Van Deursen, *Kopergeld*, III: 'Volk en overheid', 25–7.
45 Dekker, *Holland*, 33.
46 Riley, *Government Finance*, 70–82.
47 Dekker, *Holland*, 144.

IV ARTISTS' ORIGINS

1 G. Brom *Schilderkunst en litteratuur in de 16e en 17e eeuw*, Utrecht 1957, 178.
2 J. M. Montias, *Artists and Artisans in Delft: A Socio-Economic Study of the Seventeenth Century*, Princeton 1982.
3 Ibid., 177–8.
4 J. L. Price, *Culture and Society in the Dutch Republic during the Seventeenth Century*, London 1974, 137.
5 Montias, *Artists*, 149–53.
6 Å. Bengtsson, *Studies on the Rise of Realistic Painting in Holland 1610–1625*, Stockholm 1952, 34–6, 51.
7 Montias, *Artists*, 163.
8 M. J. Bok, Vraag en aanbod op de Nederlanse kunstmarkt, 1580–1700, Utrecht 1994, 189–94. During the first half of the seventeenth century the number of Utrecht artists visiting Italy had declined significantly.
9 Montias, *Artists*, 69. These figures are, generally speaking, supported by the apprenticeship premium of fifteen to eighty-five guilders – depending on the length of the apprenticeship – which R. de Jager has calculated from Dutch apprenticeship contracts; R. de Jager, 'Meester, leerjongen, leertijd. Een analyse van zeventiende-eeuwse Noordnederlandse leerlingcontracten van kunstschilders, goud- en zilversmeden', *Oud Holland* 104 (1990), 75–6. For information about the apprenticeship premium for prominent painters see H. Floerke, *Studien zur niederländischen Kunst- und Kulturgeschichte. Die Formen des Kunsthandels, das Atelier und die Sammler in den Niederlanden vom 15.–18. Jahrhundert*, Munich–Leipzig 1905, 133; G. Schwartz, *Rembrandt.*

Sämtliche Gemälde in Farbe, Stuttgart–Zurich 1985, 54.
10 The origins of the apprentices from prosperous families can be found in E. van de Wetering, 'Problems of Apprenticeship and Studio Collaboration', in J. Bruyn et al. (eds), *A Corpus of Rembrandt Paintings*, II, Dordrecht–Boston–Lancaster 1986, 56; M. J. Bok, '"Nulla dies sine linie". De opleiding van schilders in Utrecht in de eerste helft van de zeventiende eeuw', *De zeventiende eeuw* 6 (1990), 64–5.
11 *Das Lehrgedicht des Karel van Mander* (1598), ed. R. Hoecker, The Hague 1916. Valuable information on this topic can be found in the seminar paper written by one of my students, A. Heinig, 'Künstler und ihre soziale Stellung', Kiel Winter term 1989/90.
12 Montias, *Artists*, 172.
13 G. J. Hoogewerff, *De geschiedenis van de Sint Lucasgilden in Nederland*, Amsterdam 1947, 144–5.
14 Floerke, *Studien*, 135–8.
15 I. H. van Eeghen, 'Het Amsterdamse Sint Lucasgilde in de 17de eeuw', *Jaarboek Amstelodamum* 60 (1969), 66.
16 For general information about this, see Hoogewerff, *Geschiedenis*.
17 Montias, *Artists*, 350–6 (Appendix B).
18 B. Haak, *The Golden Age: Dutch Painters of the Seventeenth Century*, translated from the Dutch and edited by E. Willems-Treeman, London 1984, 30.
19 M. Stürmer, *Herbst des Alten Handwerks. Zur Sozialgeschichte des 18. Jahrhunderts*, Munich 1979 offers a good overview of the organization of artisans and guilds in early modern times.
20 Montias, *Artists*, 76–88.
21 Hoogewerff, *Geschiedenis*, 143–4.
22 Ibid., 144.
23 Montias, *Artists*, 100; on Amsterdam, see Floerke, *Studien*, 42.
24 Van Eeghen, 'Lucasgilde', 88–9.
25 Floerke, *Studien*, 43.
26 Montias, *Artists*, 100.
27 J. M. Montias 'Cost and Value in

Seventeenth-Century Dutch Art', *Art History* 10 (1987), 458. Around 1670 the share of foreign artists had been reduced by forty per cent.

28 A. T. van Deursen, *Het Kopergeld van de gouden eeuw*, 4 vols, Assen–Amsterdam 1978, II: 'Volkskultuur', 68–71.

29 Montias, *Artists*, 114.

30 Ibid., 121.

31 Ibid., 125–6. By including the other Dutch cities Montias has calculated an average painter's rent as being 133.3 guilders for the period 1654–65; J. M. Montias, 'Estimates of the Number of Dutch Master-Painters, their Earnings and their Output in 1650', *Leidschrift* 6, no. 3 (1990), 66–7.

32 Montias, *Artists*, 129.

33 Ibid., 130–3.

34 Ibid., 133–5. This included the process of emancipation in which at least some of the painters distanced themselves from the other artisanal groups; H. Miedema, 'Kunst-schilders, gilde en academie. Over het probleem van de emancipatie van de kunstschilders in de Noordelijke Nederlanden van de 16de en 17de eeuw', *Oud Holland* 101 (1987), 1–34.

35 Haak, 'Golden Age', 33.

36 F. D. O. Obreen, *Archief voor Nederlandsche Kunstgeschiedenis*, 7 vols, Rotterdam 1877–1890, V, 189–94.

37 Montias, 'Estimates', 59–64.

38 Floerke, *Studien*, 33–4, 168; A. Bredius, *Künstler-Inventare. Urkunden zur Geschichte der Holländischen Kunst des XVIten, XVIIten und XVIIIten Jahrhunderts*, 8 vols, The Hague 1915–22, VII, 102.

39 Haak, 'Golden Age', 36.

40 Compiled from Montias, 'Estimates', 61 (Table 1).

41 Ibid., 63–4.

42 Burke, *Culture and Society in Renaissance Italy 1420–1540*, London 1972, 255, 303–10.

43 Ibid., 225–7; see also p. 20 above.

44 Cited in N. Pevsner, *Die Geschichte der Kunstakademien*, Munich 1988, 90–1.

45 Cited in Haak, 'Golden Age', 32.

46 A. Houbraken, *Große Schouburgh der Niederländischen Maler und Malerinnen* (1719) ed. A. von Wurzbach, rep. Osnabrück 1970, 119; J. von Sandrart, *Teutsche Academie der Bau-, Bild- und Mahlerey-Künste* (1675), ed. A. R. Peltzer, Munich 1925, 202–03.

47 See p. 48 above.

V PATRONAGE

1 B. Haak, *The Golden Age: Dutch Painters of the Seventeenth Century*, translated from the Dutch and edited by E. Willems-Treeman, London 1984, 36–8.

2 C. W. Fock, 'The Princes of Orange as Patrons of Art in the Seventeenth Century', *Apollo* 110 (1979), 469–70.

3 G. Schwartz, *Rembrandt. Sämtliche Gemälde in Farbe*, Stuttgart–Zurich 1978, 80–1.

4 B. Brenninkmeyer-de Rooij, 'Noticies betreffende de decoratie van de Oranjezaal in Huis ten Bosch', *Oud Holland* 96 (1982), 133–90.

5 B.-M. Baumunk, ' "Von Brasilischen fremden Völkern." Die Eingeborenen-Darstellungen Albert Eckhouts', in K.-H. Kohl (ed.), *Mythen der Neuen Welt*, Berlin 1982, 188–201.

6 K. Fremantle, *The Baroque Town Hall of Amsterdam*, Utrecht 1959.

7 Haak, 'Golden Age', 360–3.

8 Schwartz, *Rembrandt*, 318–20.

9 I. H. van Eeghen, 'Wat veroverde Rembrandt met zijn Claudius Civilis?', *Maandblad Amstelodamum* 56 (1969), 145–9.

10 Montias, *Artists and Artisans in Delft: A Socio-Economic Study of the Seventeenth Century*, Princeton 1982, 183–90.

11 S. Slive, *Frans Hals*, exh. cat. Washington, London and Haarlem 1989–90, Munich 1989, 252–7.

12 Schwartz, *Rembrandt*, 143.

13 Montias, *Artists*, 195.

14 Floerke, *Studien zur niederländischen Kunst- und Kulturgeschichte*, Munich–Leipzig 1905, 64–7.

15   Ibid., 67–70.

16   A. Bredius, 'De delftsche schilders Jan Willemsz. Decker en Willem Jansz. Decker', *Oud Holland* 10 (1892), 195.

17   A. Bredius, *Künstler-Inventare. Urkunden zur Geschichte der Holländischen Kunst des XVIten, XVIIten und XVIIIten Jahrhunderts*, 8 vols, The Hague, 1915–22, I, 321–4; Montias, *Artists*, 198–9.

18   Bredius, 'Decker', 193. Floerke, *Studien*, 57.

19   Montias, *Artists*, 200–01; Details of the Laurensschen auctions also in J. M. Montias, *Vermeer and his Milieu: A Web of Social History*, Princeton 1988, 37–47.

20   See above, 103ff.

21   Montias, *Artists*, 203.

22   Floerke, *Studien*, 44–5.

23   Ibid., 49–50.

24   Montias, *Artists*, 24.

25   Schwartz, *Rembrandt*, 214.

26   Floerke, *Studien*, 34–5.

27   Ibid., 36.

28   Montias, *Artists*, 192.

29   Floerke, *Studien*, 19.

30   All these people are dealt with in detail in Montias, *Vermeer*.

31   Floerke, *Studien*, 21.

32   Ibid., 169; see also p. 118 below.

33   Ibid., 22.

34   See p. 97 below.

35   J. M. Montias, 'Art Dealers in the Seventeenth-Century Netherlands', *Simiolus* 18 (1988), 252.

36   Floerke, *Studien*, 110.

37   For this and the following see, Bredius, *Künstler-Inventare*, I, 228–39 (Renialme), V, 1660–84 (van Uylenburgh); Montias, 'Art Dealers', 37.

38   Schwartz, *Rembrandt*, 139–42 compare S. A. C. Dudok van Heel, 'Het "Schilderhuis" van Govert Flinck en de kunsthandel van Uylenburgh te Amsterdam', *Jaarboek Amstelodamum* 74 (1982), 70–90; on the following see also Floerke, *Studien*, 103–08; A.-M. S. Logan, *The 'Cabinet' of the Brothers Gerard and Jan Reynst*, Amsterdam–Oxford–New York 1979, 90–6.

39   See below pp. 113–14.

40   Montias, 'Estimates of the Number of Dutch Master-Painters, their Earnings and their Output in 1650', *Leidschrift* 6, no. 3 (1990), 69.

41   Bredius, *Künstler-Inventare*, II, 457–520; Montias, 'Estimates', 69.

42   A. Chong, 'The Market for Landscape Painting in Seventeenth-Century Holland', in Peter Sutton, *Masters of 17th Century Dutch Landscape Painting*, Exhibition in Amsterdam, Boston and Philadelphia, Boston 1987, 116 (Table 1).

43   J. M. Montias, 'Cost and Value in Seventeenth-Century Dutch Art', *Art History* 10 (1987), 456–62.

44   Chong, 'Market', 113.

45   Ibid., 117–18 (Table 3); in brackets the number of the price mentioned and the year respectively; * means that it deals with a commission from an official body.

46   Ibid., 116 (Table 2).

47   Marten Jan Bok and Gary Schwartz have contended that even in the mid-seventeenth century more than half of Dutch paintings could have been commissioned, and were mainly carried out by assistants, journeymen and copyists, whose works were sold at the lower end of the market through art dealers. M. J. Bok, and G. Schwartz, 'Schilderen in opdracht in Holland in de 17e eeuw', in J. W. J. Burgess et al. (eds), 'Kunst in opdracht', *Holland, regional-historisch tijdschrift* 23 (1991), 183–95.

VI   Collections and Collectors

1   J. M. Montias, *Artists and Artisans in Delft: A Socio-Economic Study of the Seventeeth Century*, Princeton 1982, 220.

2   W. Brulez, *Cultuur en getal. Aspecten van de relatie economie-maatschapij-cultuur in Europa tussen 1400 en 1800*, Amsterdam 1986, 55. Such estimates are naturally speculative. Thus Brulez estimates that 150,000 of the accepted output of 17 million pictures remain. In contrast, according

to Montias, less than 100 of the 40,000–50,000 pictures in Delft households have survived, Montias, *Artists*, 220.

3 A. Bredius, *Künstler-Inventare Urkunden zur Geschichte der Holländischen Kunst des XVIten, XVIIten und XVIIIten Jahrhunderts*, 8 vols, The Hague, 1915–22.

4 J. M. Montias, 'Works of Art in Seventeenth-Century Amsterdam: An Analysis of Subjects and Attributions', in D. Freeberg and J. de Vries (eds), *Art in History. History in Art. Studies in Seventeenth-Century Dutch Culture*, Santa Monica 1991, 331–72.

5 Montias, *Artists*, Table 8.3; Montias, 'Analysis', Table 3.

6 C. W. Fock, 'Kunstbezit in Leiden in de 17de eeuw', in T. H. Lunsingh Scheurleer et al. (eds), *Het Rapenburg. Geschiedenis van een Leidse gracht*, V(a), Leiden 1990, 6.

7 Compiled from Montias, *Artists*, Table 8.3.

8 Compiled from Montias, 'Analysis' Table 3.

9 Montias, *Artists*, 246.

10 Ibid., 245.

11 Fock, 'Kunstbezit in Leiden'. See also above, p. 99.

12 Montias, 'Analysis', 24–5.

13 In total, the majority of the paintings (fifty to sixty per cent) in the inventories had been painted by local Amsterdam artists.

14 Montias, *Artists*, 247–58.

15 See above, pp. 97–8.

16 Montias, 'Analysis', Table 5.

17 Montias, *Artists*, 268–71.

18 See above, p. 92.

19 An overview of the Italian collections in Amsterdam can be found in F. Lugt, 'Italiaansche kunstwerken in nederlandsche verzamelingen van vroeger tijden', *Oud Holland* 53 (1936), 97–135.

20 A.-M. S. Logan, *The 'Cabinet' of the Brothers Gerard and Jan Reynst*, Amsterdam–Oxford–New York 1979.

21 Ibid., 77–85.

22 It is difficult to reconstruct the 'Dutch Gifts' to the king. Seventeenth century paintings by Italian artists are noted as *Dutch Present* in King Charles II's inventory, even though five further paintings from the Reynst collection also went to England. However, only fourteen of the twenty-two paintings are illustrated in the *Caelaturae* and definitely became part of the collection. Logan, *Cabinet*, 82–4.

23 See above, p. 97.

24 H. Floerke, *Studien zur niederländischen Kunst- und Kulturgeschichte. Die Formen des Kunsthandels, das Atelier und die Sammler in den Niederlanden vom 15.–18. Jahrhundert*, Munich–Leipzig 1905, 167.

25 Ibid., 168; see also above, pp. 94–5.

26 H. J. Postma, 'De Amsterdamse verzamelaar Herman Becker (ca. 1617–1678). Nieuwe gegevens over een geldschieter van Rembrandt', *Oud Holland* 102 (1988), 1–21.

27 See, for example, A. Bredius, 'Nieuwe Rembrandtiana', *Oud Holland* 28 (1910), 1–5; Floerke, *Studien*, 168.

28 Postma, 'Becker', 6–7.

29 Ibid., 16-1B (Appendix).

30 Ibid., 8.

31 E. S. de Boer (ed.), *The Diary of John Evelyn*, Oxford 1935, 39.

32 A. Hauser, *The Social History of Art*, vol. II: *Renaissance, Mannerism, Baroque*, translated in collaboration with the author by Stanley Godman, London, 1962; reprinted 1992, 200.

33 Montias, *Artists*, 263.

34 W. Martin, *Het leven en de werken van Gerrit Dou beschouwd in verband met het schildersleven van zijn tijd*, Leiden 1901, 42–4; I. Gaskell, 'Dou, his Patrons and the Art of Painting', *Oxford Art Journal* 5 (1982), 15–61.

35 Floerke, *Studien*, 169.

36 On van Ruijven see J. M. Montias, *Vermeer and his Milieu: A Web of Social History*, Princeton 1988, 246–55.

37 M. J. Bok, *Vraag en aanbod op de Nederlandse kunstmarkt, 1580–1700*, Utrecht 1994, Chap. 3.

38 B. Brenninkmeyer-de Rooij in B. Haak, *The Golden Age of Dutch Painters*

of the Seventeenth Century, translated from the Dutch and edited by E. Willems-Treeman, London, 1984, 63.

39 Postma, 'Becker', 14–15 (Index of the books in the estate inventory).

CONCLUSION

1 See pp. 16–17 above.
2 L. de Vries, 'Jan Steen "de kluchtschilder"', unpublished dissertation, University of Groningen 1977, 103–06, 109–10.
3 P. Burke, *Culture and Society in Renaissance Italy 1420–1540,* London 1972, 111–14.
4 Ibid., 279.
5 Ibid., 290–1.
6 Alongside the vertical (social) mobility there was also a reduction in the horizontal (regional) mobility. Thus the passenger revenue from passenger barges (*trekschuiten*), the most important way of travelling between cities, decreased by around half between the 1660s and the 1740s. This can, on the one hand be traced back to the development of income and the economy, but on the other, mirrored the fact that both the population and economic activity was concentrated in the centres of Amsterdam and Rotterdam (to the detriment of Gouda and Delft), J. de Vries, *Barges and Capitalism. Passenger Transportation in the Dutch Economy, 1632–1839,* Utrecht 1981, 268–331; J. C. Riley, 'The Dutch Economy After 1650: Decline or Growth?', *Journal of European Economic History* 13 (1984), 563.

Bibliography

Primary Sources

Angel, P., *Lof der Schilder-Konst* (Leiden 1642), facsimile edn, Amsterdam 1972.

Boer, E. S. de, (ed.), *The Diary of John Evelyn*, Oxford 1935.

Bredius, A., *Künstler-Inventare. Urkunden zur Geschichte der Holländischen Kunst des XVIten, XVIIten und XVIIIten Jahrhunderts*, 8 vols, The Hague 1915–22.

Burney, C., *A General History of Music*, 4 vols, London 1776–89.

Court, P. de la, *Interest van Holland ofte gronden van Hollands welvaren*, Amsterdam 1661.

Defoe, D., *A Plan of the English Commerce* (London 1728), Oxford 1928.

Hoecker, R., (ed.), *Das Lehrgedicht des Karel van Mander*, (1598), The Hague 1916.

Hoogstraeten, S. van, *Inleyding tot de Hooge Schoole der Schilder-konst* (Rotterdam 1678), facsimile edn, Utrecht 1969.

Houbraken, A., *Große Schouburgh der Niederländischen Maler und Malerinnen* (1719), ed. A. von Wurzbach, rep. Osnabrück 1970.

King, G., *Two Tracts: Natural and Political Observations and Conclusions upon the State and Condition of England*, ed. G. E. Barnett, Baltimore 1936.

Mander, K. van, *Das Leben der niederländischen und deutschen Maler*, ed. H. Floerke, 2 vols, Munich–Leipzig 1906.

Miedema, H., *De archiefbeschieden van het St. Lukasgilde te Haarlem 1497–1798*, 2 vols, Alphen 1980.

Obreen, F. D. O., *Archief voor Nederlandsche Kunstgeschiedenis*, 7 vols, Rotterdam 1877–1890.

Sandrart, J. von, *Teutsche Academie der Bau-, Bild- und Mahlerey-Künste* (1675), ed. A. R. Peltzer, Munich 1925.

Temple, R. C., (ed.), *The Travels of Peter Mundy in Europe and Asia*, IV, London 1925.

Temple, W., *Observations upon the United Provinces of the Netherlands*, ed. George Clark, Oxford 1972.

Secondary Sources

Abel, W., *Agrarkrisen und Agrarkonjunktur. Eine Geschichte der Land- und Ernährungswirtschaft Mitteleuropas seit dem hohen Mittelalter*, Hamburg–Berlin 1966.

Algemene geschiedenis der Nederlanden, 15 vols, Haarlem 1977–83.

Alpers, S., *The Art of Describing: Dutch Art in the Seventeenth Century*, Chicago–London 1983.

————, *Rembrandt's Enterprise. The Studio and the Market*, London 1988.

Antal, F., *Die florentinische Malerei und ihr sozialer Hintergrund*, Darmstadt 1960.

Aymard, M., (ed.), *Dutch Capitalism and World Capitalism*, Cambridge–Paris 1982.

Baasch, E., *Holländische Wirtschaftsgeschichte*, Jena 1927.

Barbour, V., *Capitalism in Amsterdam in the 17th Century*, Ann Arbor 1976.

Baumunk, B.-M., '"Von Brasilischen fremden Völkern". Die Eingeborenen-Darstellungen Albert Eckhouts', in K.-H. Kohl (ed.), *Mythen der Neuen Welt*, Berlin 1982, 188–201.

Bengtsson, Å., *Studies on the Rise of Realistic Painting in Holland 1610–1625*, Stockholm 1952.

Bergström, I., *Studier i Holländskt Stillebenmaleri under 1600–talet*, Göteborg 1947.

Bialostocki, J., 'Einfache Nachahmung der Natur oder symbolische Weltschau. Zu den Deutungsproblemen der holländischen Malerei des 17. Jhdt.', *Zeitschrift für Kunstgeschichte* 47 (1984), 421–38.

Blankert, A., 'Kunst als regeringszaak in Amsterdam in de 17e eeuw. Rondom schilderijen van Ferdinand Bol', exh. cat., Amsterdam 1975, Lochem 1975.

————, 'Gods, Saints, Heroes: Dutch Painting in the Age of Rembrandt', exh. cat., Washington, D.C. 1980.

P. Blickle, *Unruhen in der ständischen Gesellschaft 1300–1800*, Munich 1988.

Bok, M. J., '"Nulla dies sine linie". De opleiding van schilders in Utrecht in de eerste helft van de zeventiende eeuw', *De zeventiende eeuw* 6 (1990), 59–68.

————, *Vraag en aanbod op de Nederlandse kunstmarkt, 1580–1700*, Utrecht 1994.

————, and G. Schwartz, 'Schilderen in opdracht in Holland in de 17e eeuw,' in J. W. J. Burgess et al. (eds), 'Kunst in opdracht', *Holland, regionaal-historisch tijdschrift* 23 (1991), 183–95.

Bosl, K., and H. Mommsen, 'Adel', *Sowjetsystem und Demokratische Gesellschaft*, I, Freiburg 1966.

Bouman, J., *Bedijking, opkomst en bloei van de Beemster*, Amsterdam 1857.

Boxer, C. R., *The Dutch Seaborne Empire, 1600–1800*, London 1965.

————, *The Dutch in Brazil, 1624–1654* (Oxford 1957), Camden 1973.

Bracker, J., North, M., and P. Tamm, *Maler der See. Marinemalerei in 300 Jahren*, Herford 1980.

Bredius, A., 'De delftsche schilders Jan Willemsz. Decker en Willem Jansz. Decker', *Oud Holland* 10 (1892), 193–6.

———, 'Nieuwe Rembrandtiana', *Oud Holland* 28 (1910), 1–5.

Brenninkmeyer-de Rooij, B., 'Notities betreffende de decoratie van de Oranjezaal in Huis ten Bosch, *Oud Holland* 96 (1982), 133–90.

———, 'Kunsttheorien', in B. Haak, *Das Goldene Zeitalter der holländischen Malerei*, Cologne 1984, 60–70.

Briels, J., *De Zuidnederlandse immigratie 1572–1630*, Haarlem 1978.

Brom, G., *Schilderkunst en litteratuur in de 16e en 17e eeuw*, Utrecht 1957.

Bromley, J. S., and E. H. Kossman (eds), *Britain and the Netherlands*, London 1960.

Brown, C., *Scenes of Everyday Life: Dutch Genre Painting of the Seventeenth Century*, London 1984.

Bruijn, J. R., and C. A. Davids, 'Jonas vrij. De Nederlandse Walvisvaart, in het bijzonder de Amsterdamse, in de jaren 1640–1664', *Economisch- en sociaal-historisch jaarboek* 38 (1975), 141–78.

Brulez, W., *Cultuur en getal. Aspecten van de relatie economie-maatschapij-cultuur in Europa tussen 1400 en 1800*, Amsterdam 1986.

Bürgers, W., Kunstkritik, rev. A. Schmarsow and B. Klemm, Leipzig 1908.

Burke, P. *Venice and Amsterdam. A Study of Seventeenth-Century Élites*, London 1974.

———, *Culture and Society in Renaissance Italy 1420–1540*, London 1972. Rev. edn: *The Italian Renaissance*, Cambridge 1987.

Chong, A., 'The Market for Landscape Painting in Seventeenth-Century Holland', in P. Sutton, *Masters of the 17th-Century Dutch Landscape Painting*, exh. cat., Boston 1987, 104–20.

Christensen, A. E., *Dutch Trade to the Baltic around 1600*, Copenhagen–The Hague 1941.

Dekker, R., *Holland in beroering. Oproeren in de 17de en 18de eeuw*, Baarn 1982.

Demetz, P., Defenses of Dutch Painting and the Theory of Realism, *Comparative Literature* 15, no. 2 (1963), 97–115.

Deursen, A. T. van, *Het Kopergeld van de Gouden eeuw*, 4 vols, Assen–Amsterdam 1978.

Dijk, H. van and D. J. Roorda, 'Sociale mobiliteit onder regenten van de Republiek', *Tijdschrift voor Geschiedenis* 84 (1971), 306–28.

Dillen, J. G. van, *Van rijkdom en regenten. Handboek tot de economische en sociale geschiednis van Nederland tijdens der Republiek*, The Hague 1970.

———, La banque de changes et les banquiers privés à Amsterdam aux XVIIe et XVIIIe siècles, *Third International Conference of Economic History*, V, (Munich 1965) Paris 1974, 177–85.

Dudok van Heel, S. A. C., 'Het "Schilderhuis" van Govert Flinck en de kunsthandel van Uylenburgh te Amsterdam', *Jaarboek Amstelodamum* 74 (1982), 70–90.

Eeghen, I. H. van, 'Het Amsterdamse Sint Lucasgilde in de 17de eeuw', *Jaarboek Amstelodamum* 60 (1969), 65–102.

———, 'Wat veroverde Rembrandt met zijn Claudius Civilis?', *Maandblad Amstelodamum* 56 (1969), 145–9.

Esch, A., 'Über den Zusammenhang von Kunst und Wirtschaft in der italienischen Renaissance. Ein Forschungsbericht', *Zeitschrift für Historische Forschung* 8 (1981), 179–222.

Floerke, H., *Studien zur niederländischen Kunst- und Kulturgeschichte. Die Formen des Kunsthandels, das Atelier und die Sammler in den Niederlanden vom 15.–18. Jahrhundert*, Munich–Leipzig 1905.

Faber, J. A., 'The Decline of the Baltic Grain-Trade in the Second Half of the Seventeenth Century', *Acta Historiae Neerlandica* 1 (1966), 108–31.

———, *Drie Eeuwen Friesland. Economische en sociale ontwikkelingen van 1500 tot 1800*, 2 vols, Wageningen 1972.

Fock, C. W., 'The Princes of Orange as Patrons of Art in the Seventeenth Century', *Apollo* 110 (1979), 466–75.

———, 'Kunstbezit in Leiden in de 17de eeuw', in T. H. Lunsingh Scheurleer et al. (eds), *Het Rapenburg. Geschiedenis van een Leidse gracht*, Va, Leiden 1990, 3–36.

Fremantle, K., *The Baroque Town Hall of Amsterdam*, Utrecht 1959.

Fromentin, E., *Die Alten Meister (Belgien–Holland)*, Potsdam 1919.

Gaastra, F. S., 'Die Vereinigte Ostindische Compagnie der Niederlande', in E. Schmitt et al., (eds), *Kaufleute als Kolonialherren. Die Handelswelt der Niederländer vom Kap der Guten Hoffnung bis Nagasaki 1600–1800*, Bamberg 1988, 1–89.

Gaskell, I., 'Dou, his Patrons and the Art of Painting', *Oxford Art Journal* 5 (1982), 15–61.

Glamann, K., *Dutch–Asiatic Trade 1620–1740*, Copenhagen–The Hague 1958.

Gombrich, E. H., 'The Social History of Art', in id., *Meditations on a Hobby Horse and other Essays on the Theory of Art*, London–New York 1978.

Groenhuis, G., *De Predikanten. De sociale positie van de gereformeerde predikanten in de Republik der Verenigde Nederlanden voor ± 1700*, Groningen 1977.

Gudlaugsson, S., *Ikonographische Studien über die holländische Malerei und das Theater des 17. Jahrhunderts*, Würzburg 1938.

———, *Komedianten bij Jan Steen en zijn tijdgenoten*, The Hague 1945.

Haak, B., *The Golden Age: Dutch Painters of the Seventeenth Century*, translated from the Dutch and edited by E. Willems-Treeman, London 1984.

Haley, K. H. D., *The Dutch in the Seventeenth Century*, London 1972.

Haks, D., *Huwelijk en gezin in Holland in de 17de en 18de eeuw. Processtukken en moralisten over aspecten van het laat 17de– en 18de–eeuwse gezinsleven*, Assen 1982.

Hauser, A., *Sozialgeschichte der Kunst und Literatur*, Munich 1978. (Orig. pub. 1951 in 2 vols). English edn: *The Social History of Art*, in 4 vols. Translated in collaboration with the author by S. Godman, London, 1962; reprinted 1992.

Hecht, P., 'The Debate on Symbol and Meaning in Dutch Seventeenth Century Art: An Appeal to Common Sense', *Simiolus* 16 (1986), 173–87.

——, 'De Hollandse fijnschilders. Van Gerard Dou tot Adriaen van der Werff', exh. cat., Amsterdam 1989.

Heek, F. van, 'Bloei en ondergang van de Hollandse zeventiende-eeuwse landschapsschilderkunst (1620–1670). Artistiek isolement- integratie-creativiteit. Een sociologische beschouwing', *Mens en maatschappij* 1979, no. 2, 127–43.

Hegel, G. W. F., *Ästhetik*, ed. F. Bassenge, Berlin 1955.

A. Heinig, 'Künstler und ihre soziale Stellung', Kiel Winter term 1989/90.

Hoogewerff, G. J., *De geschiedenis van de Sint Lucasgilden in Nederland*, Amsterdam 1947.

Hotho, F. G., *Geschichte der deutschen und niederländischen Malerei*, I, Berlin 1842.

Huizinga, J., *Holländische Kultur im siebzehnten Jahrhundert*, Basel 1961.

Israel, J., *The Dutch Republic and the Hispanic World, 1606–1661*, Oxford 1982.

——, *Dutch Primacy in World Trade, 1585–1740*, Oxford 1989.

Jager, R. de, 'Meester, leerjongen, leertijd. Een analyse van zeventiende-eeuwse Noordnederlandse leerlingcontracten van kunstschilders, goud- en zilversmeden', *Oud Holland* 104 (1990), 49–111.

Jongh, E. de, 'Erotica in vogelperspectief. De dubbelzinnigheid van een reeks 17de eeuwse genrevoorstellingen', *Simiolus* 3 (1968/9), 22–74.

——, 'Realisme en schijnrealisme in de Hollandse schilderkunst van de zeventiende eeuw', *Rembrandt en zijn tijd*, exh. cat., Brussels 1971, 143–95.

——, 'Tot lering en vermaak. Betekenissen van Hollandse genrevoorstellingen uit de zeventiende eeuw', exh. cat., Amsterdam 1976.

Kauffmann, H., 'Die Fünfsinne in der niederländischen Malerei des 17. Jahrhunderts', in *Festschrift Dagobert Frey*, Breslau 1943, 135–57.

Klein, P. W., *De Trippen in de 17e eeuw. Een studie over het ondernemersgedrag op de Hollandse stapelmarkt*, Assen 1965.

——, 'De heffing van de 100e en 200e penning van het vermogen te Gouda, 1599–1722', *Economisch-historisch jaarboek* 31 (1965/6), 41–62.

——, 'De zeventiende eeuw', in J. H. van Stuijvenberg (ed.), *De economische geschiedenis van Nederland*, Groningen 1977, 79–118.

——, 'Stagnation économique et emploi du capital dans la Hollande des XVIIIe et XIXe siècles', *Revue du Nord* 52 (1970), no. 204, 33–41.

Kriedte, P. *Spätfeudalismus und Handelskapital. Grundlinien der europäischen Wirtschaftsgeschichte vom 16. bis zum Ausgang der 18. Jahrhunderts*, Göttingen 1980.

Lademacher, H., *Geschichte der Niederlande. Politik-Verfassung-Wirtschaft*, Darmstadt 1983.

Larsen, E., (with the collaboration of J. Davidson), *Calvinist Economy and 17th Century Dutch Art*, Lawrence, Kansas 1979.

Logan, A.-M. S., *The 'Cabinet' of the Brothers Gerard and Jan Reynst*, Amsterdam–Oxford–New York 1979.

Lopez, R. S., 'Hard times and Investment in Culture', in *The Renaissance: Six Essays*, New York 1962, 29–54.

Lugt, F., 'Italiaansche kunstwerken in nederlansche verzamelingen van vroeger tijden', *Oud Holland* 53 (1936), 97–135.

Maddison, A., *Groeifasen van het kapitalisme*, Utrecht–Antwerp 1982.

Martin, A. von, *Soziologie der Renaissance*, Munich 1974.

Martin, W., *Het leven en de werken van Gerrit Dou beschouwd in verband met het schildersleven van zijn tijd*, Leiden 1901.

———, 'The Life of a Dutch Artist in the Seventeenth Century', *Burlington Magazine* 7 (1905), 125–8 and 416–27; 8 (1905/06), 13–24; 10 (1906/07), 144–54.

Miedema, H., 'Verder onderzoek naar zeventiende-eeuwse schilderij formaten in Noord-Nederland', *Oud Holland* 95 (1981), 31–49.

———, 'Kunstschilders, gilde en academie. Over het probleem van de emancipatie van de kunstschilders in de Noordelijke Nederlanden van de 16de en 17de eeuw', *Oud Holland* 101 (1987), 1–34.

Montias, J. M., *Artists and Artisans in Delft: A Socio-Economic Study of the Seventeenth Century*, Princeton 1982.

———, 'Cost and Value in Seventeenth-Century Dutch Art', *Art History* 10 (1987), 455–66.

———, *Vermeer and his Milieu: A Web of Social History*, Princeton 1988.

———, 'Art Dealers in the Seventeenth Century Netherlands', *Simiolus* 18 (1988), 244–56.

———, 'Estimates of the Number of Dutch Master-Painters, their Earnings and their Output in 1650', *Leidschrift* 6, no. 3 (1990), 59–74.

———, 'Socio-Economic Aspects of Netherlandish Art from the Fifteenth to the Seventeenth Century: A Survey', *Art Bulletin* 72 (1990), 359–73.

———, 'Works of Art in Seventeenth-Century Amsterdam: An Analysis of Subjects and Attributions', in D. Freedberg and J. de Vries (eds), *Art in History. History in Art. Studies in Seventeenth-Century Dutch Culture*, Santa Monica 1991, 331–72.

Munro, J. H., 'Economic Depression and the Arts in the Fifteenth-Century Low Countries', *Renaissance and Reformation* 19 (1983), 235–50.

Nierop, H. F. K. van, *Van ridders tot regenten*, Dieren 1984.

Noordegraaf, L., *Hollands welvaren? Levensstandard in Holland 1450–1650*, Bergen 1985.

North, M., *Geldumlauf und Wirtschaftskonjunktur im südlichen Ostseeraum an der Wende zur Neuzeit (1440–1570)*, Sigmaringen 1990.

———, and F. Snapper, 'The Baltic Trade and the Decline of the Dutch

Economy in the 18th Century', in J. P. S. Lemmink and J. K. van
Koningsbrugge (eds), *Baltic Affairs. Relations between the Netherlands and
North-Eastern Europe*, Nijmegen 1990, 263–86.

———, 'Art and Commerce in the Dutch Republic', in K. Davids and J.
Lucassen (eds), *A Miracle Mirrored: The Dutch Republic in European Perspective*, Cambridge 1995, 284–302.

Nusteling, H., *Welvaart en werkgelegenheid in Amsterdam 1540–1860. Een relaas
over demografie, economie en sociale politiek van een werelstaad*, Amsterdam–
Dieren 1985.

Oss, A. C. van, and B. H. Slicher van Bath, 'An Experiment in the History of
Economy and Culture', *Journal of European Economic History* 7 (1978),
407–14.

Panofsky, E., 'Der gefesselte Eros (Zur Genealogie von Rembrandts Danae)',
Oud Holland 50 (1933), 193–217.

Parker, G., *Der Aufstand der Niederlande*, Munich 1979.

Peter-Raupp, H., *Die Ikonographie des Oranjezaal*, Hildesheim–New York 1980.

Pevsner, N., *Die Geschichte der Kunstakademien*, Munich 1988.

Postma, H. J., 'De Amsterdamse verzamelaar Herman Becker (ca. 1617–
1678). Nieuwe gegevens over een geldschieter van Rembrandt', *Oud
Holland* 102 (1988), 1–21.

Postumus, N. W., *De geschiedenis van de Leidsche lakenindustrie*, 3 vols, 's-
Gravenhage 1908, 1939.

———, 'The Tulip Mania in Holland in the Years 1636 and 1637', *Journal of
Economic History* 1 (1929), 435–65.

———, *Inquiry into the History of Prices in Holland*, 2 vols, Leiden 1946, 1964.

Press, V., 'Französische Volkserhebungen und deutsche Agrarkonflikte
zwischen dem 16. und dem 18. Jahrhundert', *Beiträge zur historischen
Sozialkunde* 7 (1977), 76–81.

Price, J. L., *Culture and Society in the Dutch Republic during the Seventeenth
Century*, London 1974.

Raben, R., and R. Vermeij, 'Worteloof en cultuurhistorie. Kunstopvattingen
van Peter Hecht en Eddy de Jongh', *Leidschrift* 6, no. 3 (1990), 41–58.

Raupp, H.-J., 'Ansätze zu einer Theorie der Genremalerei in den
Niederlanden im 17. Jahrhundert', *Zeitschrift für Kunstgeschichte* 46
(1983), 401–18.

Regin, D., *Traders, Artists, Burghers: A Cultural History of Amsterdam in the 17th
Century*, Assen 1976.

Reinhard, W., *Geschichte der europäischen Expansion*, 4 vols, Stuttgart– Berlin–
Cologne–Mainz 1983–1990.

Renger, K., 'Zur Forschungsgeschichte der Bilddeutung in der
holländischen Malerei', in *Die Sprache der Bilder*, exh. cat., Braunschweig
1978, 34–8.

Renier, G. J., *De Noord-Nederlandse Natie*, Utrecht 1948.

Riegl, A., *Das holländische Gruppenporträt*, Vienna 1931.

Riley, J. C., *International Government Finance and the Amsterdam Capital Market 1740–1815*, Cambridge 1980.

———, 'The Dutch Economy After 1650: Decline or Growth?', *Journal of European Economic History* 13 (1984), 521–69.

Roorda, D. J., *Partij en Factie. De oproeren van 1672 in de steden van Holland en Zeeland. Een krachtmeting tussen partijen en facties*, Groningen 1961.

Rosenthal, Š. M., 'O nekotorych social'nych predposylkach gollandskoj i flamandskoj živopisi XVII veka. Predvaritelnye materialy k sociologičeskomu izučeniju iskusstva', *Pamjatniki gosudarstvennogo muzeja izjašěnych iskusstv* 5 (1926), 91–108.

Rudolph, H., '"Vanitas". Die Bedeutung mittelalterlicher und humanistischer Bildinhalte in der niederländischen Malerei des 17. Jahrhunderts', in *Festschrift Wilhelm Pinder*, Leipzig 1938, 405–33.

Schama, S. *Überfluß und schöner Schein. Zur Kultur der Niederlande im Goldenen Zeitalter*, Munich 1988.

Schilling, H. 'Die Geschichte der nördlichen Niederlande und die Modernisierungstheorie', *Geschichte und Gesellschaft* 8 (1982), 475–517.

Schneeloch, N.-H. 'Die Bewindhebber der Westindischen Compagnie in der Kammer Amsterdam, 1674–1700', *Economisch- en sociaal-historisch jaarboek* 36 (1973), 1–74.

———, *Aktionäre der Westindischen Compagnie von 1674. Die Verschmelzung der alten Kapitalgebergruppen zu einer neuen Aktiengesellschaft*, Stuttgart 1982.

Schöffer, I 'La stratification sociale de la République des Provinces Unies au XVIIe siècle', in R. Mousnier (ed.), *Problèmes de stratification sociale*, Paris 1968, 120–32.

———, 'Die Republik der Vereinigten Niederlande von 1648 bis 1795', in T. Schieder (ed.), *Handbuch der Europäischen Geschichte*, IV, Stuttgart 1968, 634–58.

———, and F. S. Gaastra, 'The Import of Bullion and Coin into Asia by the Dutch East India Company in the Seventeenth and Eighteenth Centuries', in M. Aymard (ed.), *Dutch Capitalism and World Capitalism*, Cambridge–Paris 1982, 215–33.

Schwartz, G., *Rembrandt*. Sämtliche Gemälde in Farbe, Stuttgart–Zurich 1978.

Slicher van Bath, B. H., *Agrarian History of Western Europe, 500–1850*, London 1963.

Slive, S., 'Realism and Symbolism in Seventeenth-Century Dutch Painting', *Daedalus* 91 (1962), 469–500.

———, *Frans Hals*, exh. cat. Washington, London, Haarlem 1989–90, Munich 1989.

Sluijter, E. J. *De 'Heydensche Fabulen' in de noordnederlandse schilderkunst, circa 1590–1670. Een proeve van beshrijving en interpretatie van schilderijen met verhalende onderwerpen uit de klassieke mythologie*, The Hague 1986.

———, 'Schliders van "cleyne, subtile ende curieuze dingen". Leidse fijnschilders in contemporaine bronnen', in E. J. Sluijter et al. (eds), *Leidse fijnschilders*, exh. cat. Leiden 1988, Zwolle–Leiden 1988, 15–55.

———, 'Hoe realistisch is de Noordnederlandse schilderkunst van de zeventiende eeuw? De problemen van een vraagstelling', *Leidschrift* 6, no. 3 (1990), 5–39.

Die Sprache der Bilder, exh. cat. Braunschweig 1978.

Stechow, W., *Dutch Landscape Painting of the Seventeenth Century*, London–New York 1966.

Stilleben in Europa, exh. cat. Münster, Baden–Baden 1979–80.

Stone-Ferrier, L. A., *Images of Textiles: The Weave of Seventeenth-Century Dutch Art and Society*, Ann Arbor 1980.

Stürmer, M., *Herbst des Alten Handwerks. Zur Sozialgeschichte des 18. Jahrhunderts*, Munich 1979.

Supple, B. E., *Commercial Crisis and Change in England 1600–42*, Cambridge 1959.

Sutton, P., *Von Frans Hals bis Vermeer. Meisterwerke holländischer Genremalerei*, exh. cat. Philadelphia, Berlin, London 1984.

———, *Masters of 17th-Century Dutch Landscape Painting*, exh. cat. Amsterdam, Boston, Philadelphia 1987–88, Boston 1987.

Tapié, V.-L., *Baroque et classicisme*, Paris 1957.

———, 'Baroque et classicisme', *Annales: Economies-Sociétés-Civilisations* 14 (1959), 719–31.

Taverne, E. R. M., 'Salomon de Bray and the Reorganization of the Haarlem Guild of St. Luke in 1631', *Simiolus* 6 (1972/3), 50–69.

Unger, R. W., *Dutch Shipbuilding before 1800. Ships and Guilds*, Assen–Amsterdam 1978.

———, 'Dutch Herring, Technology and International Trade in the Seventeenth Century', *Journal of Economic History* 40 (1980), 253–79.

Unger, W. S., 'Nieuwe gegevens betreffende het begin der vaart op Guinea', *Economisch-historisch jaarboek* 21 (1940), 194–217.

Vries, Jan de, *The Dutch Rural Economy in the Golden Age, 1500–1700*, New Haven–London 1974.

———, *Economy of Europe in an Age of Crisis*, Cambridge 1976.

———, *Barges and Capitalism. Passenger Transportation in the Dutch Economy, 1632–1839*, Utrecht 1981.

———, 'An Inquiry into the Behaviour of Wages in the Dutch Republic and the Southern Netherlands from 1580 to 1800', in M. Aymard (ed.), *Dutch Capitalism and World Capitalism*, Cambridge–Paris 1982, 37–61.

———, 'The Decline and Rise of the Dutch Economy, 1675–1900', in G. Saxonhouse and G. Wright (eds), *Technique, Spirit and Form in the Making of the Modern Economics: Essays in Honour of William N. Parker*, Greenwich 1984, 149–89.

———, *European Urbanization, 1500–1800*, London 1984.

Vries, Johan de, *De economische achteruitgang der Republiek in de achttiende eeuw*, Amsterdam 1959.

Vries, L. de, 'Jan Steen "de kluchtschilder"', unpublished dissertation, University of Groningen 1977.

Wackernagel, M., *Der Lebensraum des Künstlers in der florentinischen Renaissance*, Leipzig 1938.

Warburg, A., 'Sandro Botticellis "Geburt der Venus" und "Frühling". Eine Untersuchung über die Vorstellungen von der Antike in der italienischen Frührenaissance', Hamburg–Leipzig 1893, rep. in id., *Gesammelte Schriften*, I, Leipzig–Berlin 1932, 1–59, 307–28.

Wee, H. van der, 'De economie als factor bij het begin van de opstand in de Zuidelijke Nederlanden', *Bijdragen en mededelingen betreffende de geschiedenis der Nederlanden* 83 (1969), 15–32.

———, 'Monetary, Credit and Banking Systems', in E. E. Rich and C. Wilson (eds), *The Cambridge Economic History of Europe*, V: *The Economic Organization of Early Modern Europe*, Cambridge 1977, 291–392.

———, (ed.), *The Rise and Decline of Urban Industries in Italy and in the Low-Countries (Late Middle Ages–Early Modern Times)*, Leuven 1988.

Wetering, E. van de, 'Problems of Apprenticeship and Studio Collaboration', in J. Bruyn et al. (eds), *A Corpus of Rembrandt Paintings*, II, Dordrecht–Boston–Lancaster 1986, 45–90.

Wilson, C. *Profit and Power: A Study of England and the Dutch Wars*, London 1957.

———, 'The Decline of the Netherlands', in id., *Economic History and the Historian*. Collected Essays, London 1969, 22–47.

———, *England's Apprenticeship, 1603–1763*, London 1965.

Woltjer, J., 'Der Niederländische Bürgerkrieg und die Gründung der Republik der Vereinigten Niederlande (1555–1648)', in T. Schieder (ed.), *Handbuch der Europäischen Geschichte*, III, Stuttgart 1971, 663–88.

Woude, A. van der, *Het Noorderkwartier. Een regionaal historisch onderzoek in de demografische en economische geschiedenis van westelijk Nederland*, 3 vols, Wageningen 1972.

———, 'Variations in the Size and Structure of the Household in the United Provinces of the Netherlands in the Seventeenth and Eighteenth Centuries', in P. Laslett (ed.) *Household and Family in Past Time*, Cambridge 1972, 299–318.

Zanden, J. L. van, 'De economie van Holland in de periode 1650–1805: groei of achteruitgang? Een overzicht van bronnen, problemen en resultaten', *Bijdragen en mededelingen betreffende de geschiedenis der Nederlanden*,102 (1987), 562–609.

———, *Arbeid tijdens het handelskapitalisme*, Bergen 1991.

———, *The Rise and Decline of Holland's Economy: Merchant Capitalism and the Labour Market*, Manchester 1993.

Index of Netherlandish Artists

Pages with illustrations are indicated by italics.

Illustrations

1 Pieter de Hooch, *The Mother*, c. 1661–3, Berlin, Gemäldegalerie Staatliche Museen Preußischer Kulturbesitz. (Photo: J. P. Anders)

2 Gabriel Metsu, *The Hunter's Present*, c. 1665, Amsterdam, Rijksmuseum, © Rijksmuseum Stichting.

3 Gerrit Dou, *Young Woman with Boy at a the Window*, 1652, Karlsruhe, Staatliche Kunsthalle.

4 Population of the province of Holland 1514–1795 (from J. de Vries)

5 Anonymous, *Polder near Enkhuizen*, c. 1600, Enkhuizen, Town Hall.

6 Hendrick Vroom, *Peaceful Trading on the Indian Coast*, 1614, London, National Maritime Museum.

7 Gerard Terborch, *Deventer Magistrates*, 1667, Deventer, Town Hall.

8 Nicolaes Eliasz., known as Pickenoy, *Cornelis de Graeff*, c. 1645, Berlin Gemäldegalerie in the Bodemuseum Staatliche Museen Preußischer Kulturbesitz. (Photo: J. P. Anders)

9 Nicolaes Eliasz., known as Pickenoy, *Catherine Hooft* (wife of the politician Cornelis de Graeff, depicted in fig. 8), c. 1645, Berlin, Gemäldegalerie in the Bodemuseum Staatliche Museen Preußischer Kulturbesitz. (Photo: J. P. Anders)

10 Michiel Sweerts, *Drawing a Nude in the Studio*, c. 1656–8, Haarlem, Frans Halsmuseum. (Photo: T. Haartsen)

11 Jan de Bray, *The Eldermen of the Haarlem Guild of Saint Luke*, 1675, Amsterdam, Rijksmuseum, © Rijksmuseum Stichting.

12 Frans Post, *Brazilian Landscape with Manor House and Sugar Mill*, c. 1655, Schwerin, Staatliches Museum.

13 Gerrit Adriaensz. Berckheyde, *The New Town Hall of Amsterdam*, c. 1675, Schwerin, Staatliches Museum.

14 Relative prices of seven commodities in five-year averages 1530–34 to 1720–24 (from J. de Vries) (1–40 = price in guilders)

15 Jan Porcellis, *Warship and Fishing Vessels near the Coast*, c. 1625, Hamburg, Peter Tamm Collection.

16 Gillis van Coninxloo, *Landscape with Hunters*, c. 1605, Schwerin, Staatliches Museum.

17 Rembrandt van Rijn, *Moses with the Tablets*, 1659, Berlin, Gemäldegalerie Staatliche Museen Preußischer Kulturbesitz. (Photo: J. P. Anders)

18 Ambrosius Bosschaert the Elder, *Vase with Flowers*, c. 1620, The Hague, Mauritshuis.

19 Adriaen Brouwer, *Inn with Drunken Peasants*, c. 1625, The Hague, Mauritshuis.

20 Jan van Goyen, *View of the Haarlem Sea*, 1656, Frankfurt, Städelsches Kunstinstitut. (Photo: U. Edelman)

21 Willem Claesz Heda, *Breakfast Table with Bacon*, 1646, Schwerin, Staatliches Museum.